MINIATURE ROSES

MINIATURE ROSES

Their Care and Cultivation

SEAN McCANN

Foreword by Sam McGredy

STACKPOLE
BOOKS

ACKNOWLEDGEMENTS

Where can one possibly begin to give credit when so much information and assistance
was forthcoming during the writing of this book? The list of those to whom I am
indebted could go on and on, but the names that follow are of the people who truly gave
me their time, energy, succour, photographs and enthusiasm: Frank Benerdella and
family; Jill Bennell; Pat Berlen; Dr Tommy Cairns; Pat Dickson; Beverly R. Dobson;
Wini and Fred Edmunds; Rose Gilardi; Lt Col and Mrs Grapes; Jerry, June and Tara
Justice; David Kenny; the Kordes family; Sheila Lee; Sam McGredy; Mary and Don
Marshall; Martin J. Martin; Dorothy Michelis; Leslie Mitchell; Ralph Moore;
Harmon Saville; Ludwig Taschner; Craig Wallace; Chris and Barbara Warner; and a
whole host of other friends in England, Scotland, Wales, Canada, the United States,
Australia, India, South Africa, Zimbabwe and New Zealand. Although it seems
inadequate, I thank you all sincerely.

CONTENTS

LIST OF PLATES

Air France
Amy Rebecca
Angel Darling
Angela Rippon
Anytime
Baby Betsy McCall
Baby Masquerade
Bambino
Benson and Hedges Special
Bianco
Billy Boy
Blue Peter
Cape Hatteras
Center Gold
Centerpiece
Chasin' Rainbows
Cheré Michelle
Chick-a-dee
Cider Cup
Cinnamon Toast
Cricket
Crissy
Cupcake
Daniela
Debut
Dee Bennett
Dresden Doll
Earthquake
Edna Marie
Eyeopener
Eye Appeal

Ferris Wheel
Firefly
Fool's Gold
Galaxy
Gentle Touch
Heartbreaker
Herbie
Holy Toledo
Inner Glow
Irish Heartbreaker
Jeanne Lajoie
Jelly Bean
Jennifer
Jim Dandy
Joycie
Julie Ann
June Laver
Kiss the Bride
Ladies' View
Lady in Red
Lavender Crystal
Lavender Jewel
Little Artist
Little Flirt
Lovers Only
Loving Touch
Maidy
Majorette
Make Believe
Mandarin
Mary Hill

Maurine Neuberger
Millie Walters
Minilights
Mood Music
Moon Mist
My Sunshine
Nickelodeon
Nigel Hawthorne
Nighthawk
Pandemonium
Peek-a-boo
Peggy Jane
Petticoat Lane
Phyllis Shackleford
Pink Petticoat
Pink Porcelain
Pinstripe
Poker Chip
Portland Dawn
Rainbow's End
Red Beauty
Regine
Renny
Ring of Fire
Rise 'n' Shine
Robin Redbreast
Rosa persica
Rose Gilardi
Roseromantic
Rouletii
Royal Salute

Savannah Miss
Sheri Anne
Simplex and Oriental
  Simplex
Snow Bride
Sommerwind
Sonnenkind
Starglo
Starla
Stars 'n' Stripes
Stolen Moment
Apricot Sunblaze
Lady Sunblaze
Orange Sunblaze
Pink Sunblaze
Yellow Sunblaze
Yorkshire Sunblaze
Swansong
Sweet Chariot
Tara Allison
Teddy Bear
Timothy Berlen
Warm Welcome
Why Not
Winsome
Wit's End
Work of Art
Yellow Doll
Zwergenfee
Zwergkönigin

FOREWORD

Much as I enjoy rose breeding, I find the day-to-day plant husbandry required to make roses flourish a bore. In the days when I lived in Ireland, I used to glance at the usual run of gardening magazines and quickly turn to the advertising pages, which I found more stimulating and amusing. Then came a rather scruffy, plain black-and-white newsweek called *Garden News*, and an Irish writer called Sean McCann, who made the rose world a bit of fun. There is nothing so dull as the plain truth. My wife says the Irish can't tell it, they embellish it, add to it and make it better. And that's the plain truth. Sean does it supremely well. His *All the World's Roses* is the most interesting book on roses I know, and I browse in it, often.

So I looked forward to receiving the manuscript of this book. Sean is an amazing guy. He's done it all – he has grown roses and bred them; he writes about roses and gossips about them; and he travels extensively in roses – and it comes out in his writing. You know that this man is an authority to the tips of his Irish-green fingers. He has the ability to make the mundane seem extraordinary, and even makes you want to be a fingers-in-the-dirt gardener. If you follow his instructions, a bit of that green will rub off on you, and everything in your garden will be magnificently disease-free and super. Your minis will be bigger (or smaller) and better. You've got to believe!

That's why I know you, too, will enjoy his writing.

SAM MCGREDY
Auckland, New Zealand

I

WHERE IT ALL BEGAN

The miniature rose has come and gone, and come and gone again throughout the centuries, but at last its time has arrived – a time with hundreds of beautiful little flowers of every shape, size, hue, colour and fragrance. The red, the white, the brown and the purple, even roses with multicoloured striped blooms, are here to brighten up the world's gardens, to tumble over walls and to grow on patios and window-sills – anywhere, in fact, where a small plant can be accommodated.

Miniature roses are sold by the tens of millions from nurseries throughout the world, and since the mid-1970s they have been gathering such momentum that their introductions today outnumber those of their bigger brothers. Apart from the obvious beauty of the miniature rose, their cost puts them ahead of most garden subjects. In most gardens a miniature rose plant will last for at least 10 years, thus eliminating the cost and labour of preparing the soil and of replanting the beds and borders each year. In addition, in a world where gardens have become smaller, where condominiums, flats and town houses have no gardens whatsoever, miniature roses can provide the beauty that the world has always found in the larger varieties for which there is no longer space.

Miniature roses may have been fashionable a hundred years ago in the streets of Paris or growing on window-ledges in Switzerland, but gardeners then could hardly have envisaged a time when the little roses would greatly outnumber the introduction of big roses. Miniature roses may be small in stature, but they are big in popularity – they have been called 'nature's over-achievers'. In the United States of America the boom began in the 1970s. The trend was picked up in Europe and spread from there, and today there is hardly a country without a nursery specializing in miniatures and offering hundreds from catalogues that bring the little roses from all around the world.

The origins of the forebears of the present-day miniatures are one of the many mysteries in the world of roses that have never been adequately explained. From as long ago as the 1800s, different authorities have had their own suggestions: the roses came from Mauritius; they were always grown in France; they were exported from Britain to France as potted roses; they came from China; they were cultivated from a bunch of seeds from a larger rose. I have even heard an Australian say that they got to his country when they 'fell off the back of a passing ship', and this is probably as adequate and as likely an explanation as any.

Many authorities say that it could all have started with a species rose called *R. chinensis minima* – but many other authorities in the field of species roses say that there is, in fact, no rose of this name. It might have been started by a variety of other species roses, of which the 'Miss Lawrence Rose' or *R. lawrenceana* could have been one. Indeed, they could all have been one and the same rose. No matter how diligently you search, you have to tread very carefully when suggesting where they began. Leading modern breeder Jack Harkness put to flight many fallacies about miniature roses in his book *Roses*. He points out that, although it has been suggested that the Royal Horticultural Society's *Dictionary of Gardening* says the miniature was in Britain in 1762, the reference is, in fact, not to a date but to a plate number in *Curtis's Botanical Magazine*. Probably the only certainty is that, whatever its origins, a miniature rose was available in Britain in the first decade of the 1800s. The next time we hear of it is 40 years later, when it became a flower-shop plant, but then, as man took over the hybridizing of roses and new types began to appear among the larger roses, so interest in miniatures faltered.

The uncertainty about the beginnings of the miniature rose probably has something to do with its constant 'stop and start' story. It weaves its way in and out of the history of the rose like a mist that comes in just to disappear almost as quickly. However, there came a time when it seemed to become stabilized, and it found its place on the balconies of many European cities for which its size made it very suitable. This resurgence led to the introduction of two roses, 'Pompon de Paris' and 'Rouletii'. They are so alike – bright pink, hardy and easy to grow – that they have frequently been confused with each other, but they are not the same rose, as anyone can discover by buying a genuine plant of each. The difference is that 'Pompon de Paris' tends to grow much leggier than 'Rouletii'. It was this smaller growing rose, 'Rouletii', that actually guaranteed the existence of the miniature as a class of its own, and, as with any good story, there is a touch of romance about it.

The little pink rose arrived at a time when miniatures had once again almost disappeared from the market, and different stories of its beginnings have been passed on through history. One legend tells how it was found growing wild on a rocky crag on a mountainside; another holds that it was found buried under snow but still in bloom; while yet another says that it was spotted in a window-box at an Italian mountain chalet. Another tale says, less believably I'm afraid, that a fortune in gold was exchanged for a mere cutting, while yet another says that the only plant surviving at the time had been taken away from the village of Onneis in Switzerland by a woman who left a few days before a fire destroyed the village.

But surely the truth was written by the man who eventually introduced it, Henri Correvan.

My friend, Colonel Roulet, informed me that he had a potted midget rose bush which grew on the window-ledge of a cottage at Mauborjet [Switzerland]. He told me that the rose bush had been grown in the pot for a century, that it bloomed from one end of the summer to the other, that it was absolutely dwarf and that it had belonged to the same family for the last 150 years. He offered to give me some branches for rooting.

Correvan succeeded in propagating it and goes on: 'I realized this was an interesting variety. That was in 1917, and in 1920 we were in a position to deliver certain quantities.' The little pink rose was soon the rage of the market place, and, in consideration of his friend's find, Correvan named it *R. rouletii* or, as the name should be, 'Rouletii'. It must have had a name before that, but what it was no one knows.

It looked like a great start again, but for some 20 years the miniature rose progressed no further. Then a Dutch nurseryman, Jan de Vink, decided that he would like to use 'Rouletii' in his hybridizing plans. He began crossing plants of the little rose with the orange-scarlet Polyantha 'Gloria Mundi', a red hybrid Rugosa from 1918, 'F. J. Grootendorst', and a Hybrid Tea of unknown parentage. However, as he had a tendency to mix up the pollen, even he could not give the correct parentage of a true miniature that emerged from his seedlings. This was crimson with a white centre, and he named it 'Peon'. It was a rose that was to open a further chapter in the story of miniature roses.

A rose is nothing if it does not find its marketing man, someone who appreciates what is new or distinctive about it. Robert Pyle, then head of the still-famous Conard-Pyle rose company in Pennsylvania, was on holiday in The Netherlands, and he visited de Vink's nursery. There was only one plant in bloom (with a single flower on it) when he saw it first, but he immediately spotted its potential. He took the plant home (although one report says that the cutting was sent to him by de Vink), had it propagated, took out a patent on it and renamed it 'Tom Thumb'. He introduced it to the public in 1936 – and the arrival of the modern miniature was heralded.

Pyle did not leave it there. He followed up his hunch that miniature roses would be very acceptable in a world in which gardens even then were getting smaller all the time, and he also saw their potential as excellent pot plants. So popular did 'Tom Thumb' become that, after its first year, it had to be withdrawn from the Conard-Pyle catalogue for a year while the company built up enough stock to meet the demand. The Pyle–de Vink partnership was on its way to success. 'Tom Thumb' and subsequent varieties made a big difference to Jan de Vink. With the money from Conard-Pyle he was able to expand, build a greenhouse and begin to breed more and more roses. Even then he worked on a very small scale, raising only a few seedlings every year in the backyard of his home. Once he was backed by the expertise of Robert Pyle, he could not go wrong. The American was always on the look-out for something new for his company, and one contemporary commented: 'I've never known a man who was so quick to appreciate another person's ideas. He would pick up a thought, polish it, give it a sparkle, and often showed the originator that it was better than he knew. Then he would even go to point out what could be done with it.' That was the quality Pyle passed on to the Dutch grower. Using Polyantha roses such as 'Ellen Poulsen', de Vink produced 'Pixie', 'Midget' and then the nursery-rhyme roses, including 'Bo Peep', 'Baby Bunting' and the still wonderful 'Cinderella', which he bred from 'Tom Thumb'. The sad end to the story of Jan de Vink appeared in an American Rose Society magazine in the early 1970s. In a letter from Holland he said that he regretted that he was giving up his membership of the Society because his eyes had become so bad that he could no longer read and that he was passing all his papers over to a collection in the famous rose town of Boskoop. It was a simple little letter that deserved a better editorial reaction than to be tucked away on a back page without comment. Maybe by that time most people had forgotten that de Vink was the man who took miniature roses along the road to their first real successes.

The de Vink roses went on to catch the attention of English nurseryman and nationally known exhibitor, Thomas Robinson of Nottingham. He signed up with de Vink to sell his roses throughout Britain. Now, suddenly, everyone wanted to be in at the birth of a new race of roses. It was all a long way from the finding of 'Rouletii' in the Swiss village.

While the Dutch hybridizer was at work, so too was the Spaniard, Pedro Dot. He also had a plant of 'Rouletii' and was busily working with it and crossing it with hybrid teas. One of the earliest of his seedlings to be marketed was 'Baby Gold Star', which brought yellow into the miniature line for the first time. Dot went on to become one of the great names in those early years of raising miniatures. He also brought in 'Pompon de Paris' (which he obviously believed was a different variety from 'Rouletii') and proceeded to produce varieties like 'Perla de Alcanada', 'Perla de Montserrat' and many others. One of his finest was 'Pour Toi' (also known as 'Para Ti', 'For You' and 'Wendy'). It is such a beautiful creamy-white rose that it is not surprising that it has picked up different names wherever it has been sold.

The outbreak of World War 2 did not help the expansion of the miniatures, but when the war was over they came back into the reckoning as Meilland of France put its powerful name behind them. Meilland carried on along the same lines as Pedro Dot, and after the wonderful Hybrid Tea 'Peace', the company would surely place its little orange-red 'Starina' very highly. Since its introduction in 1965, 'Starina' has consistently been among the top miniatures the world over.

Miniature roses were not a solely European preoccupation, however. In California a young man named Ralph Moore decided to touch a rainbow. He began to breed roses in the 1930s, and where did he begin? With a plant of 'Rouletii'. Then he discovered 'Oakington Ruby', which is thought to be a sport of 'Rouletii', and from this amazing little rose he went on to produce varieties far in advance of anything that had ever been done with the miniatures. Pedro Dot, de Vink and others influenced him in the early days, but he searched out – and found – the whole race of roses that make up today's vast collection of miniatures. Among his greatest discoveries was that the 1956 Floribunda 'Little Darling' was a great producer of miniatures, and the line has been followed by breeders ever since. It would be no reflection on the other hybridizers who had gone before him to say that Ralph Moore really placed miniature roses on the map.

Most of the world's top hybridizers have said that their miniature breeding was influenced by Ralph Moore and that they were helped along the road to success by the roses he produced. This is certainly true of New Zealand's Sam McGredy, who wrote in *Look to the Rose*:

> Whenever I think of miniatures I immediately think of Ralph Moore. No one else has done so much to improve the type and to make them popular ... he had the vision and he was dreaming his dreams of minis when none of the rest of us bothered.

These comments would meet with universal agreement, and every breeder today would acknowledge that there are numerous Moore roses in their breeding lines. Certainly the McGredy miniatures – and even some of the larger roses – will find the little 'New Penny' as well as the red and white 'Stars 'n' Stripes' figuring in their parentage.

The ranks of miniature breeders are constantly finding new recruits, and hardly a year goes by without newcomers adding their names to those of Moore, McGredy, Saville, Jolly, Harkness, Dickson and the three non-related Williamses – Benjamin, Ernest and Michael Williams. All of these have helped to estab-lish the miniature firmly on the world's stage. The increase in miniature breeding has been such that in 1969 only seven miniatures were registered; within 10 years the total was 50 a year; another 10 years on and the annual registration for miniatures reached almost 70. Today whole shows are devoted to miniatures, with exhibitors travelling hundreds of miles just to show their roses. A special miniature magazine is issued, and there does not seem to be even a suggestion of a halt to the march of the little roses.

Yes, miniature roses have come a long, long way since 'Tom Thumb' made its trans-Atlantic crossing. Today you can find them in every corner of the world and in every possible type, from micro-miniatures to shrubs, ground covers and climbers that reach up to 8 ft (2.4 m) high. Their colours range from pearl pink to crazy mixtures of orange, red and yellow, while flower shapes vary from the old-fashioned quartered blooms of many petals to the pin-pointed centres of the modern rose.

There is nowhere you cannot grow a miniature, be it Alaska or Australia. If ever there was a success story it has to be that of the miniature rose.

2

WHAT IS A MINIATURE ROSE?

There is no such thing as a 'typical' miniature rose – and I am sure that we are all the better for it. Each year, as more and more miniatures appear on the market, the images that they present bring new concepts with them, so that the range today varies from tiny bushes, hand-high from the ground, to robust, shoulder-high types with flowers that stun with their beauty. As the astonishing boom in these plants progresses, it should not be a surprise to anyone that there is frequent debate about what a miniature rose should look like.

One school of thought says that daintiness is the most important attribute of the plant. But what is dainty? Unfortunately, to some it just means small, and thus many beautiful and dainty, but larger, roses are passed over. The basic judging point for a miniature rose should be that the leaves, flowers and plant should all be small – that is, smaller than the Floribunda or the Hybrid Tea – with the plant in proportion to foliage and flower. Call it a mini-version of a big rose and you might have an idea of what you should expect, but even that seemingly simple explanation is not always acceptable, as miniatures change with every year that passes. Today there are Hybrid Teas and Floribundas that grow only 18 in (45 cm) high, but these are not in proportion, as the flowers and foliage are far too big for the plant size. So they cannot be included in any definition of miniature.

It must have been easy enough to settle on the classification of the miniature rose in the mid-1900s when 'Perla de Montserrat', 'Tom Thumb' and 'Cinderella' were (and still are) among the smallest roses you could find, but as the growing and breeding of miniatures has gathered momentum, so have the bloom and plant sizes increased. This has led to frequent suggestions that miniatures should be categorized in groups, with the tinier ones being Micro-miniatures and the larger ones being labelled Patio (in Great Britain) and, even more inappropriately, Sweetheart roses in the United States and Canada. Other countries do not seem to have made up their minds. In between, breeders have suggested that other names would be more appropriate, and many of these have been patented and copyrighted by the growers themselves for their own roses. One of the first to see the possibilities of these larger-than-mini roses was J. Benjamin Williams of Maryland, who described them as 'Mini-flora', a very appropriate designation and a name that he copyrighted.

In an introduction to the miniature rose section of the American Rose Society Annual for 1988 Dr Thomas Cairns suggested three categories – Micro-miniatures, Miniatures and Macro-miniatures. This seems a reasonable suggestion, which would give a much wider appreciation of the different sizes of blooms. Ralph Moore takes the idea further by suggesting that miniatures should be numbered by size – Class 1 for the tiny ones, Class 2 for the medium ones and Class 3 for the larger flowers. Certainly either of these methods would rule out many of the other names that have accumulated around these roses – Cushion roses (for the smaller, denser miniatures), Minimo, Macrominia, Midinette and Petitflora. Unfortunately, the official name (although it is hardly ever used) for the larger miniatures was set by the World Federation of Rose Societies as 'Dwarf clustered-flowered' roses – a committee name that lacks the slightest touch of the romantic heritage that surrounds these, and, indeed, all, roses. The name also overlooks the fact that many of the new miniatures are not cluster-flowered at all but produce one bloom on each stem.

This is not a new debate. In the early years no one could decide whether the group name should be fairy, dwarf or pigmy. Then someone found the name miniature, and everyone seemed satisfied, until, that is, breeders began to take in the whole range of roses from climbers and shrubs to old garden roses and the more modern Hybrid Teas and Floribundas.

So the disagreement continues, although some changes in classification will have to come as the range of miniatures extends from small cushions to large climbers. Even among the blooms you can find flowers as tiny as $\frac{1}{2}$ in (13 mm) and as large as 2 in (5 cm). To add to the confusion, many of these larger blooms will finish even bigger if they have been grown on a budded plant rather than being grown from a cutting, and if the bloom sizes increase on budded stock, so too will the plants themselves. In plant size the range begins with some bushes that, fully developed, stay as low as 9 in (23 cm), while others can easily reach 18 in (45 cm), and the climbers, with their perfect miniature blooms, can get as high as 8 ft (2.4 m). Growing conditions will also have a bearing on the eventual size of a plant, sunshine, water and food being the basic elements that condition the growth.

The Micro-miniatures are the smallest of them all. These are tiny, generally bushy plants with a variety of flower types that range from the simple five petalled varieties to full, well-filled blooms of 30 and more petals. The smallest of all these in commerce is 'Si', with a bud that is not much bigger than a wheat grain. It was bred in Spain by Dot in 1957, and it is a robust little plant that seldom gets much bigger than 9 in (23 cm) high. Many miniatures will not grow to more than about 12 in (30 cm) high; these include 'Littlest Angel' (medium yellow), 'Little Linda' (medium yellow), 'Bambino' (pink), 'Cinderella' (white), 'Lynne Gold' (yellow), 'Tiny Flame' (coral) and one of the first roses from de Vink, the little red 'Midget'.

However, fashion has not yet come down on the side of the Micro-miniatures, and they are not among the most popular of the range. The fashion leaders are all in the mid-range size of blooms that go from 1 in (2.5 cm) to $1\frac{3}{4}$ in (4.5 cm), and the number of varieties within this group is stunning. These roses have a high-pointed flower in which the petals swirl to a pencil-sharp centre. This is a long way from the first miniatures, whose flowers were generally small, informal and composed of many spiky petals that opened out to a rosette shape. Although a number of the rosette-shaped blooms are still being introduced, they are certainly outnumbered by the more modern-shaped flower.

In a way, this movement to the high-centred flower has meant that a great number of lovely new varieties in many different shapes of bloom have been by-passed. Today, if you were to ask almost anywhere in the world for the top 10 varieties, you would be offered miniatures that conformed to this style, and the names that would be mentioned immediately would be the white 'Snow Bride', the light apricot (often more creamy) 'Loving Touch', the apricot 'Jean Kenneally', the pink to almost white 'Minnie Pearl' and the superb yellow 'Rise 'n' Shine'. But truth to tell, these roses are not just the fashionable miniatures of the day; they are among the very best for growing in any garden, pot, planter or box – and there can be no better recommendation than that. Yet all the time they are being challenged, and young pretenders are arriving by the score every year. Some of these introductions will never be seen outside some local gardens of the towns where they were raised, while others, possibly not as good, will benefit from international distribution.

Not only are the top roses being challenged by other varieties with the same bloom quality, but we have also seen the emergence of miniatures that hark back to earlier days as hybridizers search for new and acceptable shapes. The result is that now, in smaller blooms, there are cup-shaped, quartered, and long-petalled flowers – everything, in fact, for which roses have always been renowned. Most of these would certainly qualify for the description of miniature.

When you move beyond these middle-sized miniatures you are into a dangerous area. Here are the bigger varieties that have not found their true place in the world of miniatures. Many have been registered as miniatures because they were not quite big enough for the next classification of Hybrid Tea or Floribunda or because they have one parent that is a true miniature. These are the roses I referred to earlier as the Patio or Sweetheart types.

There is nothing to stop anyone calling his plant a Patio or a Sweetheart rose, and the truth is that, while the miniature reigns as king in the United States and, to a slightly lesser degree, in Canada, no one really wants to have his roses registered outside this classification. The opposite seems to have been true in Britain, where, because breeders were years behind in producing miniatures, no real market was built for them. In fact, only one company, Gregory's of Nottingham, made miniatures a large part of its production, and it dealt mainly with roses originated in California by Ralph Moore. When British growers eventually began to produce the smaller varieties, they reached instead for a new classification and called them Patio roses.

The trouble was that the flowers on the first of these roses were definitely of the miniature size. In fact, one top seller, 'Peek-a-boo', was sold through Jackson & Perkins of Oregon as a miniature under the name 'Brass Ring', and it has won many prizes in shows there and in New Zealand as a true miniature. Later introductions in the Patio division were still very much in the miniature tradition, especially in the bud stage, although their eventual bloom size takes them beyond the fashionable and accepted grading of a miniature.

Pat Dickson of Northern Ireland, one of the world's top hybridizers, was the man who introduced the name Patio roses, and he has done all he can to educate purchasers into what they can expect from his plants. His description of Patios is that they are smaller in flower, foliage and stems than the compact-growing Floribundas and should grow from 14 in (36 cm) to 21 in (53 cm). He is not worried that people may think of them merely as roses to grow on a patio or in a courtyard; he believes that gardeners will see them as multi-purpose plants, capable of being used anywhere in the garden. However, after a quick rise in the number of Patio roses in the late 1980s, there has been a definite slowing down in their appeal and production by 1991.

There is certainly a place for these in-between size roses in our gardens, and many of the new miniature gardens being opened around the world grow these side by side with the smaller roses. Among the top varieties are many produced by the pioneers of the Patio roses, Dicksons, including 'Gentle Touch', 'Sweet Magic', 'Little Woman' and 'Cider Cup'. Another top-selling Patio has been 'Sweet Dream' (syn. 'Fryminicot') from Fryers of Cheshire, although I do feel that this one looks more like a small Floribunda, especially when grafted. As a cutting it is quite a different plant.

The success of the larger than miniature roses has not been nearly as pronounced in the United States, where roses like 'Angel Darling'. 'Church Mouse', 'Yellow Butterfly', my own 'Gold Country' and 'Timothy Berlen' are still registered and shown as miniatures, even though their flowers and plants are definitely as large as the British Patios. Indeed, many of the top-rated miniatures ('Loving Touch', for example) grow bigger than the Patio roses when they, like the Patios, are grown on budded stock. If the British Patio roses were to be grown on their own roots, I am sure that many would easily fit into the miniature market.

However, as the bewilderment about the bigger 'miniatures' dies down, there is no doubt there will be an international place for these roses, and there is much more to come within this group of roses. Herb Zipper, a hybridizer from New York State, is now crossing miniatures with shrub roses, Hybrid Musks and some of the largest Hybrid Teas. The result is that his catalogue contains a number of roses that he calls 'Rubenesque', because, he says, 'I think of them as buxom beauties'. He finds it hard to equate a belief that, in the larger roses, 'big is better even if it gets a bit grotesque – but heaven help the miniature bloom that goes over an inch in diameter'. Zipper finds that, even though the larger roses are not being acknowledged officially, the general public 'adores them'. He believes that rose breeders must make use of the vast gene pool that is available and produce great garden 'miniatures' without being too concerned over either bloom or plant size.

It is a fine line of distinction and one that has exercised a lot of comment in recent years and will continue to do so as the output of miniatures – big and small – grows year by year.

Climbing Miniatures

If you want to start an argument within a group of miniature rose growers just mention that one of the first two roses responsible for the revival of these little roses was a climber and you will be swallowed up in debate. The truth is that 'Pompon de Paris' does exhibit the tendencies of a climber, especially if it is left unpruned for a year or so. Surprisingly enough, however, no real climbing miniatures have resulted from breeding with this one, and the development of this type of rose has been very slow.

Climbing miniatures received a boost in 1989, when Chris Warner, then an amateur breeder, won the coveted Gold Medal and President's International Trophy of the Royal National Rose Society in England with one of his newest varieties. Not only did he take the top prize, but just a rung or so below was another of his climbers. In his book *Climbing Roses*, Warner described what a miniature climber should be. 'Miniature climbers should have narrower stems, smaller foliage, and flowers less than 2 in (5 cm).' He could have added that they must show a real tendency to climb and not just to send up long, narrow stems that have little or no real climbing ability. His own roses grow up to 8 ft (2.4 m).

There had been miniature climbers before the Warner hybridized varieties, but they have never really made the impact they should. This was mainly because, in many climates, they just would not climb. For instance, the loveliest of them is 'Jeanne Lajoie', a rose pink, full-petalled variety that I have seen climbing in wonderful condition in California. Yet when I took it to my own garden, it never grew taller than about 4 ft (1.2 m). In California Ralph Moore grew some early climbers like the light yellow 'Jackie', 'Pink Cameo' and 'Red Cascade', although 'Red Cascade' is more suitable for a hanging basket than for use as a climber unless it is grafted, when it can make an interesting cascade. Moore has recently moved back into this area and produced 'Work of Art', an orange and yellow blend with good flower form, fragrance and the ability to get up to 6 ft (1.8 m), and he promises that there are many more in the pipeline. Other producers are looking towards the climbers, and there is a lovely white called 'Snowfall', which can reach 8 ft (2.4 m) tall. This is an area of miniature growing that could well get a big boost

from these new varieties. They make fine specimen plants if suitably tied or wired to a fence or tripod, and, being less rampant than their big brothers, they will find many a home in large planters on patios or in conservatories. There are also climbing versions of many of the bush types such as 'Rise 'n' Shine' and 'Lavender Lace'.

Ground-cover Roses

Here is a group of roses of which some fit into the miniature collection, although more and more of them have larger flowers than the initial little entrants into this area. There is an idea that the term 'ground cover' is something new among roses, but that is not so. Writing in the 1930s, that wonderful rosarian Dr J. Horace McFarland used the term about a rose he found growing in the garden of an Irish-American rose lover, W. C. Egan. Dr McFarland wrote:

It was at Egandale [Egan's home] that I saw a rose that I found had been named 'Max Graf'. It was growing in a great heap on his lawn when I first came under its influence. On that day in late June it was a mass of splendid single pink flowers amid glossy green leaves that were in themselves highly decorative. This rose, I discovered, was not of Mr Egan's origination. But it might have been credited to him as introducer because everyone who saw it wanted it. It has slipped into commerce and plants were obtainable. I pursued its origin and found that a man in Massachusetts whose name was Bowditch had combined either or both *Rosa rogusa* and *R. wichuraiana* with our splendid American native *R. setigera*. This rose was therefore an international flower. It interested me particularly because it was such a grand ground cover and, as I came to know it later, my interest grew. I found that I could grow it in about thirty per cent access to sunlight and so it now lives at Breeze Hill [his famous garden in Harrisburg, Pennsylvania, which has since disappeared].

The hybridizer was, in fact, from Connecticut not Massachusetts, and his name was James H. Bowditch. It was the hardiness, vigour and disease resistance of 'Max Graf' that made it a great ground-cover rose, but unfortunately for us, with miniatures primarily in mind, the flower is much too big to be considered in this class. But it was the first and therefore worth noting.

In more recent times the summer-flowering, Japanese-bred 'Nozomi' captured an important place as one of the first of the small-flowered ground-cover roses. Its reputation was built on the fact that it could be used effectively as a variety for a hanging basket or even as a climber. I have used it as a weeping standard or tree rose, in hanging baskets, as a clump rose along my driveway and along the top of banks or walls. It is an incredibly useful little pearly pink rose that has been joined recently by the red 'Suma'. Unfortunately, 'Nozomi' blooms fully only throughout the main summer months, but I have had flowers on a potted bush right past Christmas. 'Suma', a true repeat-flowering variety, shows that 'Nozomi' is being widely used now as a breeding rose that will bring great benefits to foliage as it is almost impervious to disease.

'Snow Carpet' is another constant-flowering ground-cover rose, although it is a little shy with the number of blooms it produces; it has tiny foliage and dainty flowers, although 'Angelita' (syn. 'Snowball') from the same breeder, Sam McGredy in New Zealand, and the English-bred 'Arctic Sunrise' do have a better flowering capacity. The French-bred 'Swany' is a mass of white flowers and has been placed at the top of many lists in places where roses have to endure very low temperatures. I once saw it nominated as one of the best roses growing in Norway, where winter-hardy varieties are really necessary.

Apart from these, it would not be fair to recommend the newer varieties of ground-cover roses as they have large flowers and a tendency to rear skywards before crashing back to earth and then trailing for long distances. However, in the next few years there will be a number of these ground-cover plants with softer foliage and smaller flowers.

Polyantha Roses

Time and time again you will be told that 'The Fairy' is a miniature rose. And so it is – in everything but official recognition. This soft pink rose was once said by a top grower to be more important to the world of roses than 'Peace'. Certainly it is a wonderful little rose but it is not a miniature; it is generally accepted as a Polyantha, a race of low-growing roses that vary in their size of bloom. They have been out of fashion for some years, but seem to be making a return, especially in the United States. Among his roses for the future Ralph Moore is breeding with 'Ellen Poulsen', which was produced in 1911 and has already given a lot to the miniature rose but may still have more to give.

Polyantha roses are distinguished by clusters of smallish blooms and by lighter than usual green foliage, which can look a little rough at times. These roses are said to have been introduced in France about 1875 with 'Paquerette', which was followed by a whole host of others, of which the pale pink and almost thornless 'Marie Pavie' is a personal favourite. The wonderful 'Ballerina', which bears continuous flowers resembling pinkish apple blossom, deserves a place in anyone's garden, whether they are growing miniature or large roses.

The classification of the Polyanthas now takes in a whole range of roses that may not be altogether accepted in the horticultural world as being truly in this group. Their main characteristics are to grow short and to bear smallish flowers, although this is not always evident in the growth. For instance, one of the prettiest and most interesting of the new roses in this group is the lavender-pink 'Yesterday', which will grow to hip height and bear bunches of lovely, airy blooms.

The other interesting example of this type of rose is the Seven Dwarf grouping. There was originally a 'Snow White', but this name was taken in recent years for a large-flowered white rose, although the original rose of this name is still available. Put the real 'Snow White' in a garden with 'Bashful', 'Doc', 'Grumpy', 'Dopey', 'Sneezy', 'Happy' and 'Sleepy' and it provides a happy corner of little roses – but don't call them miniatures, much as they may look like them.

Cut Flowers

The place of the miniature rose in the cut-flower market is being re-established by a ground swell of new interest. Purchasers of small roses find that they make ideal flower arrangements on dinner-tables where larger roses do tend to cut off the viewing area. They are so neat that they fit in just about anywhere, while the blooms have extraordinary lasting power.

In restaurants, too, these roses have a very personal attraction that lifts them above the normal run of decorative flowers. Add to that the lower freight charges for the little roses, and they can be seen to have definite economic advantages.

I recently heard from a young Italian hybridizer, Andrea Mansuino, who is carrying on a family tradition that was begun in the 1930s by his father's uncle, Quinto Mansuino. There can be no doubt that Quinto Mansuino was another hybridizer who followed his dreams. He believed there was a need for a new type of florist rose, and he set out with his own ideas to breed this important plant. He wanted to combine blooms of fine texture but half the size of the normal roses being sold in the shops with almost thornless stems that would be well balanced against the flower size. In addition, of course, the varieties must have free-flowering habits with blooms that would last a long time on the bush or when cut.

His breeding programme was intensive as he brought in a great range of different types of roses such as Teas and Hybrid Teas because of their continuous-flowering ability and their tendency to bear one flower on each stem. *R. banksiae* was brought in for its glossy leaves, slender stems and fewer thorns; *R. chinensis* 'semperflorens' for its ability to keep on flowering with lots of blooms; *R. foetida* and *R. foetida* 'Bicolor' for their bright colour; *R. centifolia* for its fragrance; *R. damascena* also for its fragrance and its strong flower stalks; and *R. canina* for its hardiness.

And the dream came true. In the 1960s Mansuino registered a rose that has been called 'Generosa' and, more often, the Mansuino Rose. It carried a small crimson flower of 30–40 cup-shaped petals, was slightly fragrant, had thin stems, dark foliage and, most importantly, bloomed profusely. It was not a miniature as we use the word today, but it was a beautiful rose in miniature and came to be labelled the Hybrid Tea miniature. This rose was, as Andrea Mansuino says, the progenitor of a strain of cut-flower cultivars grown mostly in Italy from the end of the 1960s to the present. The roses bred from this base have seldom been grown outside Italy because they did not find favour in trials in other countries, including the United States, but the blooms were highly acceptable in the cut-flower markets of San Remo, Pescia and Roma as well as in similar markets in Switzerland and Austria.

Now, however, Andrea Mansuino sees a wonderful opportunity, and he is hybridizing along the same genetic lines and producing a new and complete range of cut-flower miniatures that are finding their way to international markets. One of these has already won a gold medal at Genoa and has been selected for the 'Euroflora' award, although this was in the Floribunda classification. Andrea Mansuino knows that at last miniature roses are coming into their own in the cut-flower business because of their high and constant ability to produce flowers all year long, their vigorous growth, and the simple and practical ways in which they can be harvested, packed and shipped.

Throughout the world other growers are making the miniature a true cut-flower business. They are using many of the modern miniatures, especially those with larger, fuller, brightly coloured blooms and with long stems. South African grower Ludwig Taschner has been a leading exponent in this business, and later in this book he offers a list of modern varieties that make ideal cut flowers. Many growers of miniature roses will find that varieties in their own gardens could well be acceptable in their own locality, especially if they could be offered on a regular basis to flower shops and restaurants. The miniature is not just a garden flower – it has great potential as a small business venture too.

3

WHERE TO GROW MINIATURE ROSES

The biggest plus about miniature roses is that they will grow anywhere and under most conditions. They can be grown in tubs, in borders, in hanging baskets, in rockeries or in beds all on their own. There are miniatures that will tumble down walls, that can be pegged down to cover a bank, that can be trained up fences and that can be used to cover garden eyesores to a height of about 8 ft (2.4 m). They are also, in most cases, even hardier than ordinary roses and need far less pampering as they get on with the real business of the rose – producing a continuous round of blooms from late spring until midwinter. The flowering period can be further prolonged by potting up some plants and bringing them indoors, where they will continue to thrive when other roses are taking their annual rest.

Today miniature roses are produced by the million in countries all over the world. In some countries, notably Britain and Australia, most miniature roses are sold on budded or grafted stock, and some Californian miniatures are also sold in this way. The great majority, however, are grown from finger-length cuttings that can be sold as tiny plants within a year, and often within six months. The differences between the two are that the potted plants will be quite small and they can be bought at any time of the year. The budded or grafted plants are much bigger and stronger, arrive on bare roots and must be planted between late autumn and early spring.

The chief advantage of roses grown from cuttings is that they are small but vigorous and can, therefore, be used as pot plants before being transferred to the garden or to a larger pot where they will last for years.

Budded plants are really for outdoor garden growing. If you want to grow them on a patio you must have a large tub to give the big, flourishing roots room to grow. They do not make good indoor subjects for longer than a couple of weeks unless the strict growing conditions described later in this chapter are observed.

Both types of miniature rose require care if they are to flourish, but even more important than that is foresight. The first question that should be asked by anyone who is going to grow miniature roses is: 'Where will I plant them?' The answer is a long way removed from the reply given to the same question in the 1964 Royal National Rose Society Annual, when the late Hilda Murrell suggested:

> for the wealthy, a little garden in a secluded corner, all laid out to scale. In such a setting the bushes can be planted in sufficient numbers of a kind to make their effect; one well-known garden which is open to the public has such a small-scale model garden made on a raised platform, in front of a doll's house which is one of the attractions.

Miniatures have come a long way since then. They certainly would not be regarded as plants merely for the wealthy, and there are far more places where they can be grown than in such situations.

The first requirement is to find a good site, one that is airy, bright, sunny and well drained. This can be a whole bed, or miniatures can be planted to great effect in a rockery or in front of a border, where the small blooms can be appreciated fully. Try to dig over the site some time before planting begins. The earlier you can manage to dig over the plot the better, and a good time to begin is early autumn. If you leave it later, the messiness of trying to prepare wet soil in winter will be frustrating. Whether you are using bare-root (budded or grafted) roses or those that have been grown in pots from cuttings makes no real difference in the area to be planted, but the tiny miniatures will do better if left for some time in their pots because they are initially so small that they may be swamped in the garden.

No matter what types of miniature you are planting, however, they need the same sort of treatment. There are five simple requirements to remember if you want to grow great plants. Your miniature roses must have light, sun, water, food and a little bit of love! These five needs apply more to plants grown in the open garden as they cannot be moved than to those grown in pots, which can be moved about until you find the best site.

Giving a plant light means that it must not be pushed under the shadow of a large rose or any other plant and that it must be planted away from over-hanging trees. It is very simple when planting a rose in winter, when most trees have shed their leaves, to put it in a position that will be quite dark when summer foliage has returned. In addition, miniatures can often be lost by placing them in a mixed border when the foliage has died down, so that in summer the roses are surrounded by plants that have grown much faster and taller than ever they do. So give your miniatures an area where they will not be over-shadowed by their neighbours.

Providing sun for your roses means finding a position where they will have about six hours sunlight every day. You must not, therefore, plant them against a wall where the sun never shines, for they will just fade away and die. A minimum of six hours sun is required to really bring them to top condition, and if that sun is in the morning so much the better. If your garden does not allow for that, find a place where the roses will get as much sunshine as possible. No one has ever seen a really successful shaded rose bed.

You must keep the ground around your roses moist. If a rose wilts and dries out there is no method by which it can be resuscitated. This does not mean that roses have to stand all day long in puddles of water – indeed, good drainage is essential to good growth – but it does mean that your roses need special watering care. Roses drink far more water than is generally suspected, and the gardener who gives his roses a daily drink will be rewarded with very good plants.

Good soil is where feeding begins. If the soil is wrong there is little or no hope for success with miniature roses – or with any other plant for that matter. Many rockeries, for example, are built with alpine plants in mind, and the soil requirements of a miniature rose will be far greater than those of alpine subjects. The most suitable soil will have a pH of 6.5, but even the best soil has to be supplemented with humus and with a fertilizer such as bone, fish and blood meal and provision made for other feeding. Every gardener knows that all soil can be improved by good tilling and fertilization, and that is why the soil should be prepared well in advance of the actual planting. The more humus that can be added the better. If the soil is a good medium loam that is a great starter, but whatever sort of soil makes up your rose planting area, it can always be improved.

And where does that little bit of love come in? Right here at the end of the other four requirements, because if you have been sufficiently dedicated to find the best possible planting spot and then to feed and water your roses, you have shown the first essentials of the tender loving care that will bring you healthy plants and beautiful blooms.

Miniatures in the Garden

In the open garden the imagination can be allowed to run riot where miniatures are concerned. There is absolutely no restriction on where or how you can grow them as long as you remember to site them in good sun.

Edging for Beds and Borders

Miniatures can be particularly effective as edging to any sort of bed or border or simply along the sides of a path or driveway. As larger roses grow older they tend to become leggy and the old wood looks ugly, but this can easily be concealed by miniatures. The smaller roses can be of the same colour as the bigger ones, or you could use a contrasting shade. A complete range of colours is now available in miniatures, and finding a closely matching shade should not be a problem. The brighter, lower growing varieties should be selected here as many new miniatures can grow tall and, unless pruned properly, will themselves become leggy after a while. In my own garden I have used the vermilion-pink 'Angela Rippon' in front of a very old Floribunda, 'Korona'. Although the colours are slightly different, they look good together and complement each other's growth and flower production. In another edging experiment I have used the small Japanese climber 'Nozomi' (the word means Hope) along my driveway, and it spreads into lovely mounds of summer flowers. This particular variety can be supplemented by a new red with the same habit of growth, 'Suma', or one of the fluffy little whites, 'Angelita' or 'Snow Carpet'. I have found that the tiny pink 'Stacey Sue' or the much older 'Bambino', which is also pink, make compact plants that flower over a long period. Special care should be taken when edging old borders or beds with new roses. The old soil will be worn out and should be replaced, especially in the area in which the new rose is expected to grow.

Hedging

Hedging might sound an ambitious way of growing miniatures, but by carefully selecting a number of the bushier varieties that keep their size a very effective hedge can be grown. The hedge can be anything to 3 ft (0.9 m) high if the new Patio or Sweetheart roses, which are larger than normal miniatures, are used. In Maryland I saw a breath-taking hedge of 'Timothy Berlen', and I have used the very bright and much older miniature 'Fire Princess' as an 18 in (45 cm) high hedge. Another red, 'Galaxy', makes a formidable and eye-catching hedge, while whites like 'Snow Bride', 'Kiss the Bride' and 'Popcorn' can also be used, although you must remember that these do better in full sun.

If you are looking for miniatures for hedging, select very bushy and vigorous varieties that do not throw their new growth way above the earlier flowers. Some of the newer varieties look like double-decker buses with a layer of flowers near the ground and then another layer much higher up. For that really robust look, I find that budded or grafted plants are best. Alternatively, use plants that you have been able to

grow on their own roots for a couple of years in adequate containers. The Californian Roselings – rooted plants that have been field hardened – are also effective. For hedging, the roses should be planted about 9 in (23 cm) apart, and in one summer they will have formed their own mass of close growth. Intensive planting like this will mean that the roses do need extra feeding and watering, and at the first sign of any disease they should be given special care (see Chapter 5).

Raised Beds

Raised beds planted with miniatures are extremely effective, and the great advantage of this type of planting is that the beds are much easier to work than those at ground level. The beds can be constructed in many different places – the top of a bank that may be at eye level, for instance, or in a hollow in the top of a low wall. Patios are often surrounded by small terrace-type walls, and these are ideal for both the trailing and the upright miniatures. You can, of course, build raised beds anywhere in your garden. They can be on a patio, over a patch of concrete or a stony area, or above soil that would otherwise be totally inadequate for growing roses. There is absolutely no limit to the type of rose that can be planted here. If you are constructing something new, it is advisable to plan a corner bed, which can be planted in one eye-catching colour, allowing the accompanying straight lines to complement the rest of the garden or to be a delightful confection of all colours.

Rock Gardens

Rockeries are ideal spots for the smaller and low-growing miniatures, but the bulkier rooting systems of the budded or grafted plants are not acceptable here. The smaller bushes grown from cuttings are ideal. They fit into the whole layout of a rockery, and, used in small batches, they can provide a really eye-catching splash of colour. From the white of the aptly named 'Popcorn' or its sport 'Gourmet Popcorn', through the bright yellow of 'Rise 'n' Shine', to the almost black-red of 'Black Jade' there is a never-ending collection of lovely subjects available, and nowhere more than in a rockery will the new (and often wild) striped colouring of roses such as 'Pandemonium', 'Roller Coaster', 'Rose Gilardi', 'Pinstripe' and 'Earthquake' be more effective. Plant individual varieties in groups of three, and the effect will be wonderful. Remember, however, that rockeries and alpine gardens are generally purposely constructed of poor and gritty soil, and this is not much good for roses. You must change the soil in the pockets where the roses are to grow, putting in new, well-fertilized compost.

Beds

It goes without saying that miniature roses make wonderful bedding plants, especially if one colour is used. Trying to mix and match miniatures in a bed is asking for disaster. If you want to have a collection of different varieties, put them in a border, where the uneven growth will not be as noticeable. Bedding roses should be of one colour, although it can be effective to plant the centre with a variety that you know will grow fairly tall and to use a known low grower of a different colour in the front row or two. Apart from that, stay away from mixed beds. If you feel that you want to give height to the miniature bed, it is possible to buy tree or standard roses, which come in different sizes and can be selected to provide the required height. Such roses can be expensive, but when they are used with discretion they do give that necessary height where miniatures are concerned. An interesting tree rose to buy would be one of the small-flowered 'ground-cover' or pliant varieties such as 'Sweet Chariot', which, when budded on a tree, will provide a lovely weeping specimen. Attention should be given to the size of the flower on the ground-cover varieties; at present many of them are very big and floppy and would spoil the whole idea of the miniature bed.

Planting

If the new rose bushes arrive before you have the ground ready, they should be looked after carefully. Plants in pots will be fine, but the bare root ones should be well watered and never allowed to dry out. If there is to be a delay of more than two days, the plants should be 'heeled-in', which means putting them in soil in a place where they will be sheltered but also adequately watered until you are ready for them. Looking after your rose bush does not mean taking away the package and placing the bush in a hot cup-

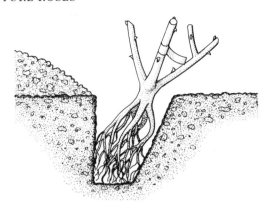

If you cannot plant a bare-root rose immediately, it should be temporarily heeled-in to prevent it drying out. Dig a sloping trench, deep enough to accommodate the roots, in a sheltered spot and cover the roots with soil, which should be firmed down with your heel. Remember to keep the rose well watered until you can plant it in its final position.

board until you are ready. That is the certain way to death, but it is surprising how many people still do it.

Roses will usually have suffered some damage to their stems or roots between being field lifted and sent through the mail. If this has happened, cut away any damaged wood and prune back to a healthy eye.

If you are using already potted miniatures for spot planting, you need only prepare an adequate hole. Do not disturb the rootball as you knock the plant from the pot but disentangle the bottom roots to allow them to move about in their new location. Make sure the hole is well dug, add some humus and place the plant so that the point at which the top growth meets the rooting section lies just below the level of the bed. Water the plant well before you place it in the ground and then, when the hole has been covered over, water it again.

One of my own rules is that you can always dig a better hole. The best hole of all will be one that allows plenty of room to fit the rootball or the long bare roots comfortably into position. This is even more important with the larger bare roots, as they generally tilt away in a different direction from the top part of the plant. Always keep the plant as upright as possible while you persuade the roots to lie in as much of a circle in the hole as you can. Gardeners often ask if the roots of bare-root plants should be trimmed before planting. There are two schools of thought about this.

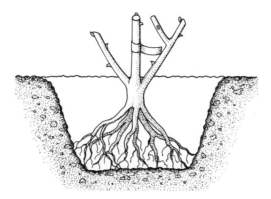

The planting hole must be sufficiently deep and wide to avoid cramping the roots and to cover the union of the top growth and rooting section.

The first is that they will grow better and quicker if they are trimmed back, provided the trimming is done carefully. A long tap-root can be trimmed back to where there is adequate hairy growth above the cut. If there is no such fine growth, you could finish up with a dead plant. The other school of thought, and the one to which I have swung over the years, is that the plant has spent almost two years in the ground building up roots and why cut them away now? I try to make the roots twist and fill the space I have provided for them instead of cutting them away.

When you are satisfied with the position of the plant and have spread the roots as best you can, begin to fill the hole with soil, making sure there are no pockets of air left around the roots. When the hole is half full, put the hose on it and fill it with water. When the water has drained away, which should happen quite rapidly, add the remainder of the soil to fill the hole, keeping the part of the budded plant where the roots meet the new growth just below ground level. Gently settle the remaining soil – do not trample around it with big elephant-like feet – and when you feel the soil has been adequately tamped in, rewater the whole area. You may have to go back and add some soil, but the task will be worth it – the well-planted bush is the happier and most productive one.

There is one vital rule about planting: never plant new roses in soil that has already been used for other roses. The soil can contain a strange disease known as rose sickness, or it can just be wasted away by the constant demands of the previous plants. If you have to plant roses in an old bed, be sure you remove enough soil from the area where the new bush is to be placed for the planting hole to be refreshed and revitalized with new soil. It is hoped that a new 'soil cleaner', Armillatox (a natural phenolic compound that is used for killing off the effects of honey fungus), will be effective and will improve the soil considerably. It is completely biodegradable and has received international acclaim. Even with this, however, it is important to add some new soil and certainly some bone meal or other fertilizer around the immediate root area.

Miniature roses are often planted along the front of an existing rose bed so that older growth on the big bushes can be hidden. If you do this, do not just push the little rose into a hole in front of the large bush. Take out the soil for your new bush, trim away any invading roots and replace the old soil with new. This will give the new bush a good start before it has to begin competing with the established rose for soil nutrients.

If your garden soil is a good, medium, well-drained loam, you are blessed. If it falls short in this respect, you must give it all the help you can. This means bringing the soil as close as possible to a pH of 6.5. It is worth buying one of the small kits for testing soil; they are inexpensive and widely available. If a test shows that your soil is alkaline (that is, it has a pH of 7.0 or higher), the acidity can be improved by the addition of more peat or flowers of sulphur, which will be transformed into sulphuric acid thus making the soil more acid. If, however, your soil tends towards acidity and is under 6.0, use lime to help correct the balance.

What makes a garden ideal for roses is plenty of humus, and this can be provided by cow, steer, horse, sheep or chicken manure. I once saw a rose garden that was at the bottom of a hill on which were sited several large chicken huts. The moisture from the houses found its way to the rose bushes, and those nearest the foot of the hill were in magnificent condition. Material from the garden compost heap can be a valuable addition, while leaf mould should not be overlooked. Gardeners in the United States look upon alfalfa pellets as one of the greatest wonders of the plant world, as they carry an enzyme that affects the plant's ability to use many soil nutrients that would normally not be readily available.

Old-time gardeners who said there was 'magic in muck' knew what they were talking about, for few gardens will not benefit from farmyard or stable manure added to the soil or used as a mulch. There are however some points to remember.

- Manure that contains straw will contain more carbon and nitrogen than other types of manure. The average balance of typical straw-based cattle manure is 0.7 per cent nitrogen, 0.3 per cent phosphorus and 0.9 per cent potassium, plus some trace elements. This will not feed a plant during the year, and the normal fertilizers will have to be added. Its value to the soil, however, is immeasurable.
- Horse manure should really be used only as a soil additive rather than as a mulch, because horses do not digest the seeds of their feed, and weed-laden gardens can result. However, the grass or oats that grow can easily be taken out by a hoe.
- Poultry manure is far richer than the normal farmyard manure, so much less is needed. It should not be used fresh.
- Sheep manure has intrigued me since I visited a shepherd's cottage in New Zealand where the roses were truly magnificent. Its value is much the same as cattle manure, but it is not easily obtained. If you live near a sheep farm look out for dags (the clippings from the rear end of the sheep that are taken away before shearing begins).
- Fish pieces should never be thrown away as they are high in nitrogen and if planted deeply enough will be a great incentive to the soil. Planted shallowly they are more likely to attract the local cats than encourage your plants to grow.
- Seaweed has a higher potash content than farmyard manure, about the same nitrogen value but less phosphate. Its main advantage is that it breaks down very quickly.

The point to remember about all manures, especially from poultry, is that they should be allowed time to rot before use. Horse manure breaks down more quickly than steer manure, but the longer all manure

can be stored the better it will be. I usually leave it from spring to autumn, when it is perfect for use, although I have successfully used horse manure a month after it came fresh from the stables. Fresh manure of any sort, however, will deprive the soil of natural nitrogen and will burn roots that come into contact with it.

The importance of providing a good planting mixture for new roses applies everywhere. I make a barrow-load of totally new soil out of a base of commercial planting mix with added bonemeal. I sometimes combine peat, sand, vermiculite or perlite, a general fertilizer and some added bonemeal, hoof, horn and fish meal (all of which supply nitrogen, phosphorus, potassium, calcium and magnesium) and, if there happens to be any available, a few handfuls of humus from the stockpile of autumn leaves. I mix this well and moisten it before use. Controlled-release fertilizers can be used in the garden, but they can be expensive for the first season, when I like to make a plant work a little for its existence. In later years applying pelleted fertilizers can be effective. With this type of planting mix your roses cannot help but get away to a splendid start, and the old soil can be moved to another part of the garden where it can continue to do a good job with any other plants.

If you live in a part of the world where cold winters can freeze the plants, you should mound up the soil around the canes, making sure they have adequate cover. Remember, too, that new roses are often planted in spring, and this can be a very dry time of the year. Newly planted roses should always be kept well watered.

Miniatures in Pots

In most parts of Europe and throughout the United States and Canada, the majority of miniatures are purchased as very small plants in 2 in (5 cm) pots. These roses will have been grown on their own roots from cuttings or through tissue culture, a method that is not as yet proving successful with larger roses but is quite successful with many miniatures. The little plants may look very puny to the untutored eye, but in one season alone they can make marvellous growth, and the finger-length plant bought in early spring will be quite a robust grower by the end of the summer.

These roses are treated differently from place to

place, but in general, the small miniatures are immediately potted on into larger containers because they are too small to be planted out in the garden. If the plants have been mailed by a nursery, they will need to be thoroughly watered to help them over the stress and dehydration of travel. I leave such plants to stand for a couple of days in a shallow tray containing about 1 in (2.5 cm) of water, and to aid revival, I add a small amount of seaweed compound or vitamin B-1. Remember, however, that the small plants should not be potted on into much larger containers where the rootball will be surrounded by a mass of wet compost; in these conditions roots will often rot away before the plants get growing. In Europe miniatures similar to these would be regarded as house plants and treated as such. They are available all the year round and are generally sold in full bloom. What many gardeners fail to realize, however, is that there is far more life in these little roses than in the normal pot plant.

Whatever your reason for buying a little rose, the plant still needs a certain amount of care. If it is purchased as a once-off house plant all it needs is water; do not soak it but provide continuous light watering, which never allows it to dry out. These plants will normally last for some weeks in average house conditions, but after that will begin to show their yearning for the great outdoors as the blooms fade and the foliage yellows.

I always find that miniatures of this type do best when planted on into a new, larger container. The size of the container is important: 5-6 in (13-15 cm) plastic pots make an acceptable new home. There is enough room for the roots to grow without being overpowered by too much water and too strong nutrients. Give them some time to harden off before putting them outside. Because they have been grown in greenhouse conditions, the plants will need a little time in a quiet, unheated spot, in a shed or in the house, while they get used to their new circumstances. After they have been growing in their new containers for a while, it is time to decide whether they should be planted out in the garden or moved into an even larger container. If they have made a lot of growth, I might even consider moving them into a 1-gallon (4.5 litre) pot, but whatever you do, do not use pots that are out of proportion to the size of the plants.

It is important to remember that miniatures growing in containers will dry out more quickly than plants grown in the open garden, so correct watering is vital. If you grow a lot of miniatures, the perfect way to make sure that the watering is correct is to use an emitter system. This is simply a hose that runs along the area in which the miniatures are growing, and from it a number of emitters deposit a steady stream of fine spray on to the plant and into the container.

When potting on, you will have to provide additional soil. Do not use ordinary garden soil, which may contain pests, bacteria and weeds that will not do your potted roses any good at all. If you are not going to pot up a lot of miniatures, many good commercial potting mixes are available that will take the guesswork out of the job. Look out for one that specifically mentions roses. The alternative is to make your own mix, which can be of peat, vermiculite or perlite, and some loam or soil pellets to give added weight. Sand can be used instead of the vermiculite or perlite, but it can become very soggy, so use it with discretion. The main problem with a peat and vermiculite or perlite mix is that it is very light, and pots can be easily knocked over, although they can, of course, be moved much more easily. Peat alone dries out very quickly. My advice is not to experiment too much with different mixes but to use the same mix for all your pots unless you have to change for any reason. By using the same potting mix throughout, your watering over the whole range will be consistent.

It is a good idea to put a layer of broken crocks or medium sized stones over the essential drainage holes at the base of a large pot to allow for better drainage. Above the crocks, I put approximately 1 in (2.5 cm) of peat, which helps to absorb large quantities of moisture and so prevent dehydration should you forget to water a plant for any reason.

The commercial mixes all have added nutrients, but a home-made mix will require the addition of a general fertilizer. The use of fertilizers has been made much easier by the introduction of controlled-release pellets, which can be incorporated into a mix without the need to add other fertilizers. If the nitrogen content of these formulations seems high, remember that it has to support vegetative growth over a long season.

After its first season in a pot, the miniature will

need a food renewal. This is better administered by granular feeding than by a powder, which can often get on the foliage and cause burning. Again, the slow-release fertilizers are a great advantage, and whether you use them or the granular type just make a few holes around the rose with a pencil-sized piece of wood and drop in the fertilizer.

The pots themselves will require some annual care. Carefully take out the balled plant and lay it gently on a bench. Inspect the roots. If they are white and look healthy, all is well. If they are black and wizened-looking then something is amiss. Inspect the pot for any signs of weevils (these eat away the roots) or other bugs. It may be that the plant has just been neglected and not fed or watered properly. If it looks as though it has outgrown its stay in the pot – that is, if it is a mass of roots with nowhere to go – it should be potted on into a larger container with more soil around it. While the pot is empty, wash it thoroughly and dry it before using it again.

Before repotting small cuttings, remember to harden off small new plants by allowing them to settle into their new environment. Then begin to expose them to lower temperatures. Keep them in their new situation for about a week and during that time ease off the amount of water they are being given, so that the outer roots in the small pot become somewhat drier. After transplanting into larger pots, begin watering again and add a vitamin B-1 or seaweed formula to help them avoid transplant shock. Do not plant them out in the garden until they have had time to expand their root systems and become well settled. In moderate climates container-grown roses can be left outside all year long, but in areas subject to heavy freezing they need to be brought into shelter when temperatures begin to drop below (20°F) (-7°C).

Advantages of Container-grown Miniatures

The most obvious advantage of container-grown miniature roses is that they can be moved around the garden. My own method is to have a number of plants hidden away at the bottom of the garden, and as they come into flower I move the pots closer to the house and take away the faded ones until they bloom again. Potted plants can also be used as temporary spot fillers in the garden. If a plant fails, just take your miniature, pot and all, and drop it into the ground, covering

it with a thin layer of soil. You should, however, make a note to lift the pot at the end of the season, or the plant will deteriorate. There is, of course, nothing to stop you just dropping the plant from the pot and putting it permanently into the soil.

Growing a plant in a pot also gives you a good chance to evaluate it before you decide where it will be best in the garden, and this is becoming more and more necessary as the height and spread of each miniature varies considerably, while the feeding, spraying and weeding of a container-grown specimen can be monitored far more easily than specimens planted in the garden.

If you are as greedy for new roses as I am, potted miniatures take up far less room and can be accommodated in many places where you could not grow ordinary roses. They can be lifted high on a bench, stool or table so that the flowers can be easily enjoyed, but having said that, I must stress that the smaller the container the more quickly the plants will dry out. Container-grown plants do need more attention than those planted in the ground. Indeed, they are completely dependent on the gardener for food and water, and watering especially needs careful monitoring.

Miniatures can bring gardening within the range of the handicapped or disabled. The plants can be potted and tended on a table or bench where they can be reached from either a chair or a wheelchair. In this way, even gardeners who may have only limited mobility can have all the enjoyment of making new small plants from cuttings (see Chapter 6) or even of hybridizing their own totally new varieties (see Chapter 7). Many of the new miniature roses are practically thornless, which makes them ideal subjects for children.

Miniature roses will continue to grow well in containers for many years if care is taken to ensure that they have not become pot bound. If they do become too big for their containers, they can easily be moved into something of a more acceptable size. Just make sure that the rootball is kept as intact as possible and that suitable new potting soil is added.

Containers

What kind of container is best for miniature roses? In truth it does not seem to matter, but I would advise against buying any container with a narrower neck than base. A few years ago I bought some of these and found it is almost impossible to extract the plant without tearing away the whole rootball. The only way to use these containers – and they are often very attractive – is to leave the plant alone, keep it well watered (daily) and fed (about twice a year). If the plant is pruned, it should continue to grow effectively for quite a long time.

The more decorative types of pots are generally the clay or terracotta type, and they are also the top-sellers for patios. They have a number of advantages over plastic pots; for instance, they keep the roots warmer in cold weather and cooler in warm weather, and they also absorb a lot of moisture and so help the roots. On the other hand, there is always the possibility that they will be blown over and broken. Clay and terracotta pots can also crack in severe frosts, and you should look out those that carry a long frost-proof guarantee. Do not be tempted to buy seconds from a potter unless you are going to use them indoors, because these are usually the first to crack in a hard frost.

Wooden containers (especially redwood) are also highly effective. Old cider, whiskey, beer or wine barrels make very attractive containers, but do make sure that these have not been carrying anything that might be poisonous to the plant. One year I bought a barrel to sink in the ground as a small pond, but the wood had been soaked in whiskey for so long that the fumes lingered for weeks! A taste of the water even showed that it was still quite alcoholic.

Almost anything that will hold soil will make a good container, but it must have adequate drainage holes. You will find that gardeners use everything from plastic pots to heavy-duty buckets, and even, in some cases, tin cans. Personally, I draw the line at the tin cans as they get very warm in just a few minutes of full sun. They also rust easily, and the stain can spoil clean paving. Large strawberry planters, with the miniatures falling down around the sides, can also be quite effective. For a more decorative style, use an old wheelbarrow, a large old boot, a watering can that may have sprung a leak and even an old tyre that has been painted.

Where you decide to show off your miniature rose will dictate what sort of container you use. A patio will require something more than a left-over coffee tin, and it is here that wooden and plastic tubs come into their own. The problem with the plastic containers is that they do not weather and age as well as natural materials – they always tend to look new before they eventually split and look tatty. Softer colours will help reflect light and help to maintain a more even temperature. Window-boxes make acceptable planting places, whether they are made of solid stone or lighter plastic. I buy many of the 6 in (15 cm) wide plastic trays, which come in various lengths and which can be left standing around the patio and are easy to move if need be. The advantage of these long trays is that they can be mulched and will hold moisture longer than a single pot. Roses, especially those that have been bought as bare-root specimens, need to be planted in a tub if you envisage leaving them in a permanent spot, but it is quite acceptable to vary the plants by dropping them in their smaller pots into the larger container. They can then be extracted and replaced when the flowers have faded.

If your garden is exposed to high winds, the containers will need something to hold them down; large stones in the base will generally be adequate. Wide, squat pots, big enough to hold four or five plants, have the necessary stability to withstand most gale-force winds.

Miniatures as House Plants

Hoping that an ordinary miniature rose bought over the counter will live happily in normal home conditions as a house plant is a vain dream. Some varieties, it is true, may live longer than a couple of weeks, but the length of time will depend on such factors as heat, light, watering and feeding and whether the plant is subject to any fumes. Place your miniature on a window-ledge or in a conservatory where it will get sun for part of the day but will not be burned away in blistering heat. If you are hoping for an extended life for the plant, then special conditions that provide good light, humidity, moisture and a temperature in the range of 60– 70°F (15–21°C) will be necessary.

The instructions for potting on roses given earlier in this chapter should be followed meticulously here. Soil that is rich in humus will give good growth, strong roots and a plant that is in better condition to withstand the stresses it will meet in its new surroundings. If the plant you buy is already potted it will not need feeding immediately, but an early infusion of some seaweed fertilizer or fish emulsion will help it adjust to its indoor environment. Keep the plant well fed with a soluble fertilizer added regularly to the water, and it will live quite happily through one or two flushes of bloom.

It is useful to remember that flushing out the pot with ordinary water without any additives will clean away any build-up of salts. If you are afraid that your tap water may contain too many unwanted salts, use distilled water instead. When the plant has finished flowering it needs to rest outside for a while, but do make sure that you do not ignore its watering needs although you should ease off the fertilizer until new growth begins. If you do not have a suitable place outside, move it to a window where it will still get light but will also get a little rest. The plant will come into bloom again and can be brought back from its temporary home as soon as you see the first suggestion of new buds. All you will need to do after that is to make sure that it is potted on into a larger container as it grows bigger. Remember to give your miniature roses room to grow.

If a passion for miniature roses really gets hold of you, they can be grown under artificial lights in any part of the house. Many people use their basements or spare rooms. Miniatures require lots of light, so special grow-lights will be needed. These should be placed about 5 in (13 cm) above the tops of the plants, and you will need a minimum of four 40-watt, broadspectrum tubes, about 4 ft (1.2 cm) long if you have the space. Place the tubes side by side and about 3 in (7.5 cm) apart, although they can be further apart if you are supplementing natural light. If you can, put reflective materials around three sides of the planting fixture. These will be of great benefit to the roses and help to encourage basal breaks rather than just top growth. If you suspend the light fixture on chains, you will be able to raise it as the plants grow. Alternatively, place extra lifts under the pots and take them away as the plants get near to the lights. Use a timing switch to operate the lights so that the plants get at least 12 hours of light each day.

Create a mini-climate around the plants to provide humidity and heat. One way of doing this is to stand the plants over a container of gravel or perlite that is kept constantly moist. Do not stand the plants directly on the gravel or in water, or the roots will be encouraged to grow out of their pots. Mist the plants regularly and watch out for the main problem of indoor roses, spider mite. Whitefly, too, can be troublesome, especially if they are allowed to build up. Spraying water with some force under as well as over the foliage will go a long way towards discouraging the spider mite, if it is done regularly. If you do use insecticides indoors, take extra precautions.

Bob Wingard of Lexington, South Carolina, has worked out the perfect set-up for his miniatures on these principles, and he finds that 14 hours of light a day is best for his plants. He, too, has occasional trouble with mildew and spider mites, and, as he dislikes using insecticides in the house, he has put his career as a pharmacist to good use by coming up with an ingenious way of keeping the mites at bay. If he catches them early enough, he says, he can deter them by simply rinsing the plants with water. If they get away, however, he uses a mix containing a shampoo used for head lice. He dips the plant in the solution several times, and because it is a shampoo, it already contains a detergent that helps to spread the material over the leaves. This could be used against spider mites outdoors as well. Wingard has not been able to find a combination that is effective against mildew yet, but when he sees an affected leaf, he just picks it off and isolates the plant from the others.

Even when they are kept indoors, plants will still need a resting time. This is usually after they have flowered for two cycles of bloom, but a keen grower will always have other plants coming along to take their place. This is best done by growing plants for indoor use from cuttings and keeping them in the same environment right from the day they are struck.

4

CULTIVATION

It has been said that, as miniature roses are only half-size roses, you need only give them half the attention that their larger brothers require. Nothing could be further from the truth.

Pruning

For some strange reason the subject of pruning roses strikes fear into the hearts of many new gardeners – and many older ones, too – and when the conversation moves on to the pruning of miniature varieties, it often induces a glassy-eyed panic. It is true that pruning miniature roses can be a fiddly job. After all, you have to look into the heart of a bush that may be growing to only ankle height and then decide what to cut away.

One day, of course, you will hear about, or even meet, the gardener who takes out an electric hedge trimmer and cuts the tops off all his miniature roses without referring to any pruning rules. A patch of balding stumps left in the ground is the only evidence that lovely little bushes once grew there. 'There,' he will say triumphantly, 'that is how it is done.' I have heard this story recounted time and time again, and I do believe that it happened. In fact, I have seen it done. But the person who did it was a commercial grower who was cutting back great areas of roses that were to be sent off to customers who would themselves complete the job according to the rules. If you were to adopt this approach with established roses you would be asking for trouble – and you would get it. Using a hedge trimmer might work for a couple of years, but after that you would have a rose bush that was a mass of dead wood and spindly growth and probably diseased as well.

Perhaps it would be a good thing to forget the word pruning altogether. Call it an annual tidy-up for the bushes and treat it as that. Regard it as you would a hair-cut – something that has to be done if only to tidy up the fringes. But whatever you call it, remember that this cutting back and tidying-up is both essential and commonsense. Dead foliage can be taken away, and nests for bugs and insects and diseases can be eliminated. You can dictate how the bush should grow: if you want a large bush, you can give the stems a medium trimming, but if you want to keep it shorter, you can cut it back more tightly. If you want to prevent stems growing over a pathway, for instance, you can cut them away there and then. This annual tidy-up is an opportunity to cut away old, diseased and broken wood and to shorten long stems so that they will produce breaks that will in turn give lots and lots of bloom. It also prolongs the life of your plants and keeps them looking young.

If you were to leave a miniature bush alone and never cut it back, it would grow and, initially, produce some blooms. As time went on, however, it would produce only a mass of small, spindly growths and miserly flowers, instead of lusty shoots and quality blooms. Trimming concentrates life into the stems of a rose. It does neither the grower nor the plant any good if the plant has to fight against decay and disease and growth that produces no results.

For me there is only one time for this annual tidy-up – early spring, although in some parts of the world – southern California, for example – late winter would be more correct. The right time to prune does vary widely depending on climate, but basically it should be when the sap begins to move in the plant. In very cold climates this will be when major freezing conditions are over. Although a heavy frost will not damage newly pruned bushes, it can wipe out any new growth. So curb your impatience and wait for the first real signs of spring. If you do find some new growth on your bushes when you go to them, cut below this to prevent the growth being killed by later frosts.

If you want to have flowers for a certain date or to bring small plants along indoors or in greenhouse conditions, you will have to guess the appropriate time. Remember that it takes some 10-13 weeks after pruning for flowers to be available. Remember, too, that you must not leave new growth exposed to heavy frost, so plants for early flowering will have to be kept under cover.

Pruning should be done when the bush is just coming out of its winter rest; then, as the sap begins to rise, it will find its place near the top of the stem to push out the new growth. If possible, pick a dry, mild day when there has not been frost and there is unlikely to be any for the next 24 hours. Even if a frost does arrive then, it won't bother the miniatures – they are little toughies at the bottom of things.

One of the real problems facing growers is that the stems are so small that the accuracy of cutting always suggested for large roses is not easy to achieve. If you cannot see an eye, leave the plant alone until the new foliage appears, then, if there is dead wood above the first foliage, you can simply trim it away.

The first essential for pruning is to have a pair of good and very sharp secateurs or clippers. They must be very sharp to make a clean cut and avoid bruising. My own favourite is the parrot-type cutter, which can get into the smallest and most awkward spots. The anvil type is harder to work in the centre of a small bush. Gloves are essential too, but for miniatures you will not need heavy-grade ones unless you have some of the very thorny varieties – most, thankfully, have minimal thorns and prickles. A kneeling pad is useful and bring along a small trowel and fork in case there are any weeds embedded around the roots.

The first step is to cut away part of the bigger stems so that you can see what is in the rest of the bush. Cut the stems back to an outward-facing eye (eyes are those spots or nipples that appear on the stem where there will be or has been a leaf axil). Try to choose an eye that points outwards, so that you can keep the centre of the bush open, but it is less essential to have the centre of a miniature bush open than in a large bush because of the configuration of the little bush, which can look less than attractive with the whole middle cut out and only new growth on the sides.

Next, take away all spindly wood that will never be strong enough to carry a good bloom. Cut it out right to the base, and do the same to any wood that is too old. Remember that you want to keep the bush looking youthful, so remove any gnarled old wood at the base, which will not produce a decent bloom anyway. If the bush has been growing for a few seasons there will also be some dead wood, and this too should be cut right out. If any stems look sickly – a light lime colour – cut them back until you get into solid green wood and again cut to an outward-facing eye.

When you are making the cut, try to make it slantwise about $\frac{1}{4}$ in (6 mm) above the eye, but do not be too worried about being exact as you can always sort it out later on. For the present, cut the stem at the height from which you want the bush to grow on, and then wait until growth begins, when you can trim back further if necessary.

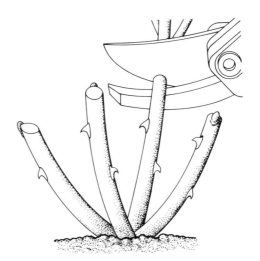

When you prune your roses, remove all dead and spindly wood and cut the flowering stems back to an outward-facing eye to help keep the centre of the bush partly open.

And that, essentially, is pruning. But don't rush away from the plant just yet. While you are down there on your knees, clean away any debris that you have left as well as any weeds that you can see. Then scuffle the soil around the bush ready to receive a handful of fertilizer later on.

This applies to roses in the ground or in a container. The only difference is that you can take your container-grown roses indoors and carry out the work on each one. But whatever you do, do not regard pruning as an unpleasant chore.

Feeding

One of the most frequently heard pieces of advice about miniature roses is that they should receive only half the feeding of normal roses. The argument is that, if they are overfed, the bushes will produce gross, out of character blooms. This is a theory with which I do not totally agree, but I must add that it is easy to become careless about a feeding programme by adding a little too much too often.

When it comes to feeding miniature roses you must consider the different requirements of the two types – the own-rooted ones and the budded or grafted ones. The deep-rooted plants, which are those that have been budded or grafted, need deep feeding, while the feeding roots of own-root bushes will be quite close to the soil's surface. Both kinds, however, need fertilizing at the same rate as ordinary roses, and if you only half-feed either type you will end up with half-quality blooms on half-quality bushes. You must keep to the quantities suggested on the fertilizer packet. An extra 'little spoonful just for luck' will cause more problems than anything else. Much more harm is done to roses by overfertilizing than by underfertilizing, but underfertilizing causes problems when gardeners take the 'half strength' theory too much to heart – not only do they halve the amount of fertilizer but they double the time between feedings. That is a diet on which many miniatures perish.

But do you know what you should be giving your roses? Let us begin with the fertilizer packaging. All fertilizer containers have the percentages of nitrogen, phosphorus and potash listed on them in that order. Nitrogen produces vegetative growth. If plants have too much, they produce lots of foliage and poor flowers; regular small amounts are much better than one great meal at the beginning of the season. The roots and the blooms get their boost from phosphorus, but too much produces small foliage and a hard, brittle plant. Sulphate of potash (not muriate of potash) stimulates general health and will give you a plant that is better able to stand up to the stresses of the season. Too much, however, will harden off the growth so that new growth finds it hard to bloom. That is why you need a good balanced fertilizer. Some plants might love a formula that gives you the proportions of nitrogen, phosphorus and potash as 0-20-20, but for a rose that would be disastrous. You should look out for fertilizers that offer nutrients in minimum proportions of nitrogen, phosphorus and potash of 5-6-12.

The debate about the relative value of organic and inorganic fertilizers in the garden is endless. The difference between the two is simply that organic materials – manure, compost of all types, alfalfa pellets and so forth – release their nutrients slowly. They have to decompose before the benefits become available to the plant. Organic materials are vital in any garden if the soil is to do its job. Inorganic – that is, chemical – fertilizers become available to the plant almost immediately. The alternative to chemical feeding is to use one of the meals, such as bone, fish and blood or seaweed, in either soluble or broken-down form. Roses will not be able to tell the difference, but they will probably notice that they have a longer wait for mealtimes if you use only organic fertilizers. Use both types, and if you have to err, do it on the side of the organic material, which can hardly ever be overused.

It has been suggested that, because humans do not go without food in winter, the same should hold good for roses. In most parts of the world, however, roses do go into a winter hibernation, a period in which they are totally inactive. This is their resting time when they do not need feeding. You would be feeding the water table, not your roses, although a survey carried out in Texas a few years ago revealed that winter feeding gave definite growth and possible hardiness benefits. My own view, however, is that the time to apply fertilizers is when the ground begins to warm up, which may be slightly after the first suggestions of bursting buds have been spotted on the canes. As soon as growth begins, feeding should start. If you put fertilizer on the ground before there is enough warmth to move it, it will just sit there and do nothing.

If you want a quicker return from your roses than nature intends, you can hurry them along by applying a soluble fertilizer to the root zone. The old-fashioned cow tea, made by placing a cloth bag full of manure in a tub of water, is still a great plant pick-me-up that has tended to get lost among the arrival of so many new packaged fertilizers. Generally speaking, the first fertilizing should be gently spread around the root area of the bush and then, just as gently, hoed in. Look around for the best bargain in rose foods, and remember that the rose will not notice the pretty picture on the label.

During the growing season, from pruning time until the middle of autumn, I give about three base fertilizer feeds to bushes – those in the ground get the same treatment as those in containers and in between I rely on foliar feeding. I would never use cow tea as a foliar feed, but there are many very good products available, and I believe that foliar feeding results in many fine rose bushes. A rose does indeed need good roots to grow successfully, and foliar feeding cannot be the only way to keep a rose bush growing well, but it does get to the point of growth immediately and feed the foliage and the blooms. There are many different formulations on the market, so select carefully. Some are more suitable for tomatoes than roses as the nitrogen content is almost fatally high. The best time to give a good foliar feed is in the roses' early growth, when the buds have formed.

Watering

No matter how much you fertilize, your roses need water, and they need more than a little dribble here and there that will just wet the top soil. You must give your roses a good, deep watering that gets right to the roots.

There are many ways to make sure your roses are watered, ranging from elaborate automatic systems to the good old watering can. If you can afford a built-in watering system with an automatic timer, your work load will certainly be lessened but you will miss a lot from not visiting each bush regularly. Watering by hand, whether it is from a hose or a can, does give you the opportunity to make sure that nothing unusual is happening to your bushes. A good water wand or hose attachment will be of great benefit in taking the pressure off your back but still allowing you to get around to see what is happening on the ground.

Watering requirements will vary from place to place. In hot climates it will have to be done every day and each bush will need 1 gallon (4.5 litres); in other climates watering may be regulated by the amount of rainfall. You must bear in mind, however, that a couple of showers once or twice a week will never give your roses enough water, and even in countries with good rainfall, such as Britain, New Zealand, Ireland and the Pacific Northwest of the United States the water needs of roses can be overlooked to the detriment of the plants.

Miniatures in containers need far more care than those in the ground, and the smaller the pot the quicker it will dry out. If a pot does dry out it should be left standing in water for several hours to recover.

I tend to vary my watering routine according to the needs of particular plants. If a plant seems to be in need of special care, I will give it a couple of gallons of water (9 litres) from a bucket that may have had some soluble fertilizer added to get right to the root zone. You can see the difference in a day or so. Sometimes I use a hose-end diluter, but I have recently come to the conclusion that this can be a very expensive way to feed and water roses.

In the long run a good watering system is a sound investment, and even a permanently laid hose with holes that allow some water to dribble on to the ground for a time every day can produce great dividends from the little plants.

Mulching

After planting, roses should be left to establish their home site in the garden. This means that, generally speaking, they should not need feeding until midsummer at the earliest because they have already been provided with a good planting mix. They should, however, also be provided with a good mulch. A mulch is not just for the rose's benefit; it also eases the gardener's work considerably as it keeps down weeds, holds in the moisture, moderates soil temperatures, encourages strong growth, provides winter protection and, finally, makes the garden look more acceptable. The perfect mulch can be found in forests, where years of leaf litter have left a carpet that is nature's way of keeping the tree roots in good shape.

A mulch is simply any deep covering of a material that will benefit the garden, and the deeper it can be, the better. Over the years I have seen mulches made from almost everything from shredded paper to top-grade carpeting, and I even saw a man pulling away at an old hair mattress and spreading it over his rose bed. More conventional mulching materials include wood chips, straw, manure, spent hops, peat moss and garden compost. Inorganic mulches – plastic, for instance – can also be used, but these cannot be later worked into the soil, and they usually look rather ugly as they flap about in the wind, so they should be avoided. There are literally dozens of materials that can provide a good mulch, and most of them, because they are organic, will need replenishing annually.

All mulches will help in the summer working of your garden, but do remember that you should put them on the ground before growth begins, otherwise you will find that they damage new, low growth. If you live in an area where winter protection is needed, you may have to consider putting down a deeper mulch. There is a legitimate theory that although mulches help to keep warmth in the soil, they also harbour diseases and insects. Despite the drawbacks, however, a garden that is mulched will always look in good shape. You must remember that mulching will provide nothing more than minimal fertilizing for your roses, or for any of your other plants for that matter. Every rose bed and every rose bush needs its own fertilizing through the years if you are to get the real benefit from the plants.

Winter Care

It is not a myth that miniature roses are often more winter hardy than their bigger brothers. But the question always remains: how hardy is hardy? Unfortunately, hardiness varies from variety to variety. The original little plants like 'Rouletii' stand up to amazingly cold temperatures, but as we move further and further away from that plant in terms of breeding so the plants' hardiness diminishes.

The best way to express cold for miniatures is to say that if you experience lengthy periods of temperatures under 20°F (−7°C) any miniature plants in the ground should be covered and those in pots should be removed to shelter. If and when you have to wrap miniatures up against freezing temperatures, their size makes the task much easier.

The main problems for the grower of miniature roses are heavy frosts and freezing conditions and cold winter winds, especially if these occur after new growth has started. If this does happen, it is often necessary to reprune all plants and remove the tender new growth that has been hit by the cold.

In Britain there is no need for extra care with miniature roses, although it would be helpful to place container-grown plants in a sheltered spot where they will be protected from the heaviest frosts and coldest winds but where you will remember to water them. Areas in which they need constant care and attention are mid- to eastern Europe, Canada and anywhere in the United States where the temperature falls to 23°F (−5°C). A new plant hardiness zone map has been issued for the United States, Canada and Mexico, and this will certainly help any gardeners who have doubts about the extremities of their weather.

It is important to maintain moisture in the canes, so before roses are put to bed they should have a good watering. It has been suggested that a little fertilizing should be done with this winter care in some of the colder areas. Lay a light covering of leaves around the bush and scatter some bonemeal over it; this is slow acting and will help the roses come back to life in spring.

But protection is the name of the game, and the amount your roses will need will depend entirely on where you live. Styrofoam boxes provide very effective cover for the extremities of North America's weather. These boxes, made from sheets 2 in (5 cm) thick, can be used for any length of bed. They can be put into place along the sides of the beds before winter approaches, and as soon as bad weather is forecast the tops can be put on. The boxes are held in place by stakes. If you have only a few miniature roses, Mini Rose Kones are effective, although they are rather large, and your roses may need some other form of covering inside them.

'Be prepared' is the vital phrase as far as miniatures in colder climates are concerned. As soon as the first phase of winter or late fall threatens to bring freezing conditions and cold, cutting winds, miniatures should be mounded over with leaves, hay or straw and

text continues on page 113

Air France
Informal blooms on a good
disease-resistant bush. A
perfect variety for pot growing.
Also known in the United
States as 'American
Independence'. (E. Ulzega,
courtesy Meilland & Cie)

Amy Rebecca

The deep yellow, non-fading blooms of this 1987 variety from Rosehills Farm are a good shape. The rose deserves everything good that has been said about it, although there are those who still say it grows too tall, even though its introducers call it a 'tiny plant' – it obviously depends on where you live. It does not, however, have exhibition shape.

Angel Darling

Each flower has 10 ruffled petals with golden stamens and an eye-catching bloom, but the question is: is it really mauve or red-mauve or lilac-red? Just one of those games that many of these little roses play when they get into a different light. Whatever the colour appears to be, this is an attractive rose.

Angela Rippon
A favourite in Britain's garden for a number of years, and deservedly so, it may not be the best-shaped rose in the book but its flowering ability, compact growth, good health and the showy, loosely petalled blooms give it a top place in any collection that I would make. Also known as 'Ocarina' and 'Ocaru', it is hardly sold at all in the United States, possibly because it is not as easy to root as most varieties, although as a budded or grafted plant it takes a lot of beating. I am not alone in believing it is one of the best miniatures anywhere to date – from South Africa Ludwig Taschner, himself a leading grower, agrees totally.

Anytime
An appropriately named miniature, it was originally to be called 'Tick-Tock', but the registration authorities would not accept the name. 'Anytime' seems to be in flower whenever you look at it. To say that the blooms are coral-orange is not completely fair, because hidden close to its heart there is a slight lavender shading that is being brought out by Ralph Moore in new varieties.

Baby Betsy McCall
This is a real little beauty that could be classified as a Micro-miniature and is just about ready for classification as a golden oldie. It came from Dennison Morey in 1960, but it still retains its place against all the more illustrious newcomers.

Baby Masquerade
Despite all the new miniatures that have appeared in recent years, here is one of the very best, and it is still going as strong after 35 years. The yellow blooms eventually turn to pink. It should not be left out of consideration where a good bedding variety is needed, although it does need a little help against mildew.

Bambino

In the context of miniature roses, this superb little pink variety is old – it came from the Spanish breeder Pedro Dot in 1953. It is low growing, bushy, tough, very disease resistant and believes that its reason for growing is to bloom.

Benson and Hedges Special
A big name for a small rose,
which is also known as
'Dorola'. When it was first
introduced, it was specially
raised and looked very small,
but when it went on general sale
as a budded plant it quickly
attained the extra few inches
that makes a Patio or
Sweetheart variety. It has good
flower quality and colour, and
can be used as a cut flower.

Bianco
A Scottish-bred Patio variety, this is a small rose, although bigger than a miniature, that produces a heavy crop of blooms.

Billy Boy
This new offering from Ralph Moore has small, very evenly coloured red flowers, vigorous growth and fine foliage. It would be suitable for those who would like a brighter flower than 'Born Free'.

Blue Peter
Unfortunately, this rose is closer to purple than blue, but it was named for a popular British television programme. It is also known in Europe as 'Bluenette'. It is a vigorous grower.

Cape Hatteras
A rose that is really chasing the crown of the best white show miniature, this was getting rave reviews long before it came on the market from Dennis and Suzy Bridges in 1988.

Center Gold

A rose that is one of the real 'biggies' among the miniatures – in every way. The bush can grow tall and the flower can grow large, but when you get the flower right you have perfection. The blooms are usually pure yellow, although now and again a pure white bloom appears, showing just a touch of red on the petal tips. Do not allow the colour or the size to deceive you – it is a very good variety.

Centerpiece

Robbie Burns may have had a rose like this in mind when he wrote 'My luv is like a red, red rose'. Here is perfection of bloom. The flowers are carried one to a stem, they are slow to fade, and they always grow well enough to produce a fine bouquet.

Chasin' Rainbows
The sparkling colours were
made famous by 'Rainbow's
End', which also came from
Harmon Saville. 'Chasin'
Rainbows' is a Micro-miniature
in the same vibrant colours.
(Sheila Lee)

Cheré Michelle
The softest shade of pink with a
lighter reverse gives only an
impression of this Jolly-bred
rose. It carries neat sprays and
is a real pastel eye-catcher, too.

Chick-a-dee
One of the tiny minis, 'Chick-a-dee' is slightly larger than the lovely 'Cinderella', and the clear, soft pink bloom sometimes carries a white stripe. It is a neat, bushy and fragrant variety. (Sheila Lee)

45

Cider Cup
Exhibitors will love the perfect flower shape, even though the rose is a little too big for the real miniature lovers. It began its show career auspiciously with a King award in the miniature court at an Ohio show in the autumn of 1990. The superb cutting blooms are borne on an enthusiastic bush.

Cinnamon Toast
I love this brownish colouring and the very well-shaped blooms that are carried on long, good cutting stems. The plants do need extra attention and care if they are to thrive.

Cricket

Bright tangerine-orange flowers are produced in a very neat head of three to four blooms. The variety came from Jack Christensen when the firm of Armstrongs was still big in the United States. It responds well to most situations with good repeat flowering and is generally healthy, although there have been some reports that it must be watched for rust.

Crissy
This little rose, which dates from 1979 when it was introduced by Leslie Strawn, never really got the appreciation it deserves, and out of all the miniature nurseries is only stocked at two. (Sheila Lee)

Cupcake
Looking just like freshly iced pink cupcakes, the blooms are perfectly formed in the Hybrid Tea manner. It was number one miniature in Australia in 1989 and was the one winner for amateur breeder Mark C. Spies in the three years from 1975 when he planted 2,150 seeds. From the moment he found the flower it took six years to get it on the market, but it was well worth the wait.

Daniela
This is one of the recent offerings from Kordes in Germany, as European breeders all began to look at the prospects offered by miniatures. A vigorous growing little variety that should not be overlooked. (Kordes)

49

Debut

A miniature from France that won the All America Rose Selection award for 1989, 'Debut' has an informal flower shape, but it goes on and on producing blooms over an extended period. If you are looking for colour and vigour and disease resistance, this is one to consider.

Dee Bennett
This orange blend rose from
Harmon Saville honours one of
the great ladies of American
roses, the hybridizer Dee
Bennett. It seems set to meet
the highest standard
(Sheila Lee)

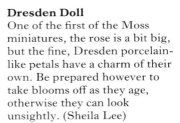

Dresden Doll
One of the first of the Moss
miniatures, the rose is a bit big,
but the fine, Dresden porcelain-
like petals have a charm of their
own. Be prepared however to
take blooms off as they age,
otherwise they can look
unsightly. (Sheila Lee)

Earthquake
This sizzling confection of
stripes lives up to its name. As
Ralph Moore says 'it will shake
up any visitor to the garden'. It
got its name immediately after
an earthquake hit the town of
Coalinga, which is close to the
Moore nurseries in California.
There is now also a climbing
version. (Sheila Lee)

Edna Marie

A rose that was named for Mary Marshall's mother; Mary already had a rose named for her and another for her husband Don. The petals are pink-tipped, fading to whitish, making this a most attractive rose. It is a very good grower, even if it does not receive all the attention it deserves. The American Rose Society review of roses lists it as a very good hedging variety.

Eyeopener

An exciting ground-cover rose from Interplant of Holland, 'Eyeopener' has bright flowers. Its habit is spreading, and it can grow to about 18 in (45 cm) high and 3 ft (0.9 m) wide.

Eye Appeal
This red cluster-flowered variety with a spreading habit carries abundant, uninterrupted blooms all season from last frost to first frost. It is a relative of the very popular 'Eyeopener', and comes from Peter Ilsink of Interplant in Holland.

Ferris Wheel
Looking perfectly wonderful here in its full yellow garb, this rose does, at times, take on some pinkish tinges so that it is registered as a yellow blend. When it is grown in warm, shaded situations the real yellow breaks through.

54

Firefly
An orange blend that actually enhances its colour as it ages, unlike most roses, which tend to fade. 'Firefly' has glossy foliage that stays healthy, and the 80-petalled flowers really catch the eye. The bush has a neat growing habit. (McGredy)

Fool's Gold
Although it bears a really superb flower with great shape, 'Fool's Gold' unfortunately leaves big gaps between its flowering spurts, and it is also a little tender in the winter. It is such a lovely thing, however, that the wait is worth it. (Dr Thomas Cairns)

Galaxy
If you called this the ever-blooming red hedge rose you would not be far wrong. Unfortunately, there are two types of rose with this name, both from Ralph Moore, but one was developed from a rogue cutting and does not have the same glow or velvet red of the real thing. Its garden display is almost year-long.

Gentle Touch
This was one of the first roses to receive the unofficial classification of 'Patio rose', but what does it matter what it is called as long as it is beautiful? This is a very pretty, soft pink rose that begins with a small, elongated bud that opens to a flower at least $2\frac{1}{2}$ in (6.5 cm) wide. It was Rose of the Year in Britain in 1986.

Herbie
The very good Hybrid Tea form of this rose from the late Dee Bennett makes it a potential show winner. However, you should be prepared for it to grow slightly taller and often to bear bigger blooms than you might expect.

Heartbreaker
One of the first miniatures to come from the association of Tom Carruth with Weeks roses, this small pink blend rose is busy and floriferous. (Sheila Lee)

57

Holy Toledo
Attractive and unusually coloured blooms that make very good cut flowers. The disadvantage of this bush is that it has a tendency to grow leggy. (Dr Thomas Cairns)

Inner Glow
This bright, well-foliaged rose is a good grower. It came from newcomer Laurie Chaffin in 1991. (Sheila Lee)

Irish Heartbreaker

Although it is leggy and pliant, 'Irish Heartbreaker' has more of a shrub effect than of a climber. The Indian red colouring has the merest touch of yellow at the heart of the bloom. It was originally sold as 'Heartbreaker', but the name had to be changed when another rose officially picked up the name first. The new name was selected by June Justice.

Jeanne Lajoie

One of the best of all the climbing miniatures, this scented grower will easily reach 5 ft (1.5 m). Although it is registered as a medium pink, it has almost a touch of mauve in it, too. I took this photograph in a shady part of a Californian garden where the colour really glowed. This is a rose that does not deserve to be ignored, and it even grows well where it does not get all the attention it deserves.

59

Jelly Bean
A Micro-miniature that is as
bright, as colourful and as neat
as a jar of Presidential jelly
beans.

Jennifer
A tall rose with pink blooms that sometimes have a light touch of mauve, this is a real grower. Pinch out the shoots to stop it growing too tall; the flowers always stay neat and well-shaped, coming as singles or in small sprays. It will form a spreading bush.

Jim Dandy
A rose with bright red and yellow blooms and great bud shape that opens quickly. It loves the heat.

Joycie
The well-shaped, bold and bright orange rose gets top marks for form and its disease-free foliage. It was named for a former member of the American Rose Society staff, Joyce Schimschock.

Julie Ann
A vigorous rose with lots of orange-red bloom, it is good for arrangements but does need help to fight off mildew.

June Laver
Canada's offering to the
miniature rose world is one of
the most perfectly shaped
blooms you will find in a colour
that is also hard to emulate.
The flowers are slow to fade
and are perfectly formed, while
the plants are hardy and
compact. If the stems that
produced these gorgeous
blooms were just a little longer,
the variety would be as close to
a 10 out of 10 as you can get.
(Sheila Lee)

Kiss the Bride
A candelabra spray of blooms
that hold a good shape in bud
and then open flat with lively
yellow stamens.

Ladies' View

This rose was named for a spot along the beautiful Lakes of Killarney where the ladies used to go to view the lakes in bygone days. The bloom opens with an almost concertina-like effect, and although it fades, it does so with some charm.

Lady in Red

Trusses of about six blooms on long stems make ideal decorative blooms. 'Lady in Red' has enough form to make it an exhibition flower. When it is grown in the sun it settles into a full red, but in the shade it will have a definite silvery reverse.

Lavender Crystal
Here is a Japanese-bred, many-petalled, well-shaped, ruffled variety that is probably as close to blue as you can get. It also carries the fragrance of most roses with this colouring. (Sheila Lee)

Lavender Jewel
It seems strange to call this rose an old timer when it has only been around since 1978, but maybe it is because it is such a prominent variety that almost everyone has it. The flowers are a fluffy confection of pure lavender, and the foliage is slightly grey tinted.

Little Artist
This is a small rose in the series that Sam McGredy called his 'hand-painted' varieties because each bloom looked different. 'Little Artist' has an attractive colour, grows well and is fragrant – even an artist could not provide much more. (Sheila Lee)

Loving Touch

This light creamy apricot has been right at the top of the miniature list for quite a while. It is a great growing bush, but as soon as it is budded or grafted it tends to grow as big as a Floribunda. Despite its great showing as an exhibition variety, it frequently carries a dropped centre, so you have to wait until the flower opens to the three-quarter stage to see it at its best. It is a good greenhouse cutting subject.

Little Flirt
This 1961 introduction is
getting old in the bloom now,
and it has been swept aside in
the United States by the tide of
new roses. But there are still
people in the world who grow it
– especially in Britain, where it
figures in the catalogues of most
growers. It can be leggy, but
when the bush is kept well
pruned it keeps its good looks.
The flowers are red, yellow-
eyed, bold and bright.

Lovers Only
It is marvellous when people
say nice things about a rose that
you have hybridized, and I have
been receiving a lot of nice
comments about this one for
some time, especially from
gardeners who suffer from the
ravages of spider mite. This
variety is said to be able to fight
off the little mites, and although
I have no idea why it should be
so, it certainly is a bonus.

Maidy
This German-bred red blend
rose never made it to the
United States or Britain, but it
is to be found in most other
European catalogues as well as
in India and South Africa.
Someone is missing something
pretty. (Kordes)

Make Believe
A darkish colour, which has been called red-purple, and a mauve blend, combine to make a really eye-catching bloom that goes white towards the centre. The flower is a little big, but that has not stopped it having a great following for those who like the flattish, open blooms that hold their shape very well. The colour does tend to fade. (Sheila Lee)

Majorette
The French firm of Meilland produced this low-growing variety. It is red to begin with, but as the flowers fade they take on a red-white striped effect, which makes the plant very effective as a low-growing bush and very useful for growing in a container.

73

Mandarin
It is difficult to decide if this new German miniature from Kordes is an orange blend or a yellow blend. It is a tallish grower and bears lots of informal flowers. (Kordes)

Mary Hill
Here is a rose that will make a very good garden or container miniature and produce lovely cutting blooms that will hold their soft blended colours right from bud to open bloom. (Sheila Lee)

Maurine Neuberger
This perfectly shaped, quickly accepted red miniature comes from Ray Spooner of Oregon. It began its career with some show wins and has gone on and on, gaining ever-wider acceptance for its super, all-through red colour. (Sheila Lee)

Millie Walters
From the Ralph Moore breeding lines, 'Millie Walters' is a cross of 'Little Darling' × 'Galaxy'. It carries well-formed blooms with reflexing petals in a good colour. The bush grows well and is generally healthy. (Sheila Lee)

Minilights
Some call 'Minilights' a ground-cover rose, others call it a Patio rose, but for me it is a truly attractive miniature, with primrose-like flowers that gather on a very low-growing but prickly bush. It lights up its spot in the garden.

Mood Music
This is a peachy-orange mossed miniature that does tend to grow rather bigger than most. Although it is not always the most vigorous of the Moss roses, it is healthy with upright growth. (Kordes)

Moon Mist
Here is a rose with the right bloom shape, a classical form and a light touch of pink at the heart of each bloom. It grows to about 12 in (30 cm), although, of course, it will grow much taller if grafted or budded. (Sheila Lee)

My Sunshine
This perfectly named rose bears flowers of the brightest yellow you can find. Each bloom has only about seven petals, but they open to perfection whatever the weather and always attract attention.

Nickelodeon
You will scarcely believe the number of blooms that this very new little rose can give. It will not be widely available until 1992 but is one to look out for: it is bright, it is unusual, and it is just about a blooming wonder!

Nigel Hawthorne
This variety is included simply because it is so beautiful. It is, in reality, a shrub and an unusual one at that, being one of the breakthroughs by Jack Harkness into the *R. persica* kingdom and showing its darker eye at the bloom centre. A spreading, prickly rose with very small, single blooms, it is one for the collectors. (Harkness)

Nighthawk
Here is a big award winner with the richest of velvet red blooms and a classic, high-pointed centre. It grows into a tallish bush. (Sheila Lee)

Pandemonium
A perfect novelty in the two most difficult colours to combine in a rose – red and yellow – 'Pandemonium' is bushy, attractive and sure to be a talking point in any garden. Named 'Claire Rayner' in Britain. (McGredy)

Peek-a-boo
Pat Dickson of Northern Ireland gave this pretty rose as nice a name as you could find, but when it got to the United States, the name was changed to 'Brass Ring'. Why, I'll never know. It is called a Patio rose, but it is small enough for any miniature show anywhere, even when it is budded or grafted.

Peggy Jane
I have no idea why this variety
blooms so well for me,
especially as I have heard others
say its problem is that it is a shy
bloomer. It is said to be a sport
of the famous 'Starina', but it
does not have the same eye-
stopping shape as that great
French rose.

Petticoat Lane
One of the roses produced by
the husband and wife team,
Dawn and Barry Eagle in New
Zealand, this clear pink variety
has won a lot of friends in its
own part of the world but has
not yet been picked up
anywhere else.

Phyllis Shackleford
This rich orange and fragrant rose was named for a lady from Texas whose enthusiastic contribution to the American Rose Society over a number of years was always greatly appreciated. (Sheila Lee)

Pink Porcelain
The flowers of 'Pink Porcelain' have just the slightest touch of soft pink suffusing the centre of the almost white blooms. An early variety from Dee Bennett, it has achieved wide popularity. (Sheila Lee)

Pink Petticoat
For long a favourite in the United States and New Zealand, 'Pink Petticoat' is beginning to pick up many friends in Britain. It is a thoroughly reliable variety that fits more into the in-between size than the true miniature group. But who cares to what size the plant grows when it gives so many good flowers? (Sheila Lee)

Pinstripe

The good double blooms of 'Pinstripe' change colour all the time; sometimes they are almost full red with a few white stripes, at other times they are all white with just a few red stripes. It is a very good variety, being tough and bearing lots of flowers. (Sheila Lee)

Poker Chip
A classically shaped Hybrid Tea bloom in a combination of brightest scarlet-orange and deep yellow make this Saville-bred miniature a much sought after variety. (Sheila Lee)

Portland Dawn
You might want to know why an Irish-bred rose is carrying an American name. The rose was, in fact, introduced to celebrate the centenary of the Portland Rose Society, the oldest in the United States. It is – even though I say it myself – a hardy, disease-resistant and colourful variety.

Rainbow's End
A variety that produces a profusion of yellow and red flowers in a perfectly shaped bloom, this is a rose that will do different things in different places – for instance, it will be yellow in a cool, shaded spot but will take on a deep shade of red if it is grown in sunshine. It is healthy, and the bushy growth means that it makes a good subject for individual or cluster planting. (Sheila Lee)

Red Beauty
This is a beautiful bloom with just a hint of yellow at the base. It does need special attention when diseases are around, especially if mildew is in the garden.

Regine
The only winner of the Award of Excellence of the American Rose Society for 1990, this lovely pink blend comes from avid exhibitor and amateur hybridizer John Heffner of Indiana. It is sturdy and softly impressive in colouring. (Sheila Lee)

Renny

This is a low-growing, upright and bushy plant that emerged from hybridizing work on 'Renae', a highly perfumed, almost thornless climbing variety that was introduced in the 1950s. Both were bred by Ralph Moore, but unfortunately 'Renny' did not pick up the fragrance of its parent, although it makes up for it with its very pretty blooms. (Sheila Lee)

Rise 'n' Shine

The timeless yellow variety is still hard to beat. It bears beautiful buds and is free-flowering, vigorous and as healthy as they come. 'Rise 'n' Shine' may send out long midseason shoots, but these should be pinched back before they become too tall. It may also be sold as 'Golden Sunblaze'.

Ring of Fire
A very impressive, vibrantly colourful newcomer that is as vigorous as you can get with a flat-opening, pompon type bloom that has good staying power. It will make a very good garden variety and was very quickly picked up as a potential for the cut-flower trade.
(Sheila Lee)

Robin Redbreast

Once you have seen this little five-petalled red rose you will have to grow it. It is bushy, very low growing and produces so many great blooms that it is ideal for growing in the garden or in a container. The clusters of bloom are a magical sight. You will probably find it listed under ground-cover roses or even as a shrub, but it will harmonize very well with miniatures.

Rosa persica

The name should probably be *Hulthemia persica* or *R. berberifolia* or even one of half a dozen others; it may be better for us all if it was just called the Persian Rose. It is included here because the blooms are small and the red eye is something that breeders would love to bring into roses whether they be miniatures or shrubs. It is a dream that has been almost achieved by Jack Harkness with some first generation hybrids.

Rose Gilardi

A delightful variety that is mossed with a profusion of soft prickles. It is a bushy, vigorous rose that carries striped flowers that are deep red and white in the sunshine but much lighter in colouring in the shade. Named for a young enthusiastic San Franciscan rose grower, who is also a District Director of the American Rose Society. (Sheila Lee)

Roseromantic

Kordes produced this white miniature flower on a shrub-like bush in honour of the World Federation of Rose Societies that met in Baden-Baden in 1983. It will cover a large area very quickly, and it fits into the ground-cover miniature category as well as the shrub classification. Be prepared to give it lots of space. (Kordes)

Rouletii

This is the rose that marked the beginning of the modern miniatures. It has since been overtaken by newer varieties, but it still has a charm all its own. (Sheila Lee)

Royal Salute
One of the first miniatures to be introduced by Sam McGredy, 'Royal Salute' has, surprisingly, never gone beyond the shores of England! I cannot find it recorded as being sold anywhere else, which is a pity because it is a bright rose red and a very good garden variety.

Sheri Anne
One of the pillars of modern rose breeding, this very decorative little rose has a touch of yellow on the reverse of its petals and makes a mockery of those who say that they find roses hard to grow. It is mother and father to dozens of our modern little roses.

Savannah Miss
It is great to be able to welcome a new rose breeder, especially when she is able to produce interesting new varieties. Laurie Chaffin from southern California produced this one for the family nursery, Pixie Treasures in Yorda Linda. The apricot blend has shape and good colouring, and it grows well. (Sheila Lee)

Snow Bride
This is one of the most widely grown roses in the United States – frequently topping the best in show and the best in garden awards. It comes from the Jolly family, and it will grow in marvellous sprays of absolutely perfectly shaped blooms.

Simplex and **Oriental Simplex**
These two little wonders of the single-flowering variety came from different hybridizers – Moore bred the original white one, while Ernest Williams in Texas came up with the orange-red with the bright yellow eye. The white variety does tend to get leggy but can be cut back quite hard. Both are vigorous growers and are well worth garden or container space, and, as you can see from this picture, they look well together. (Sheila Lee)

Sommerwind
This German-bred shrub, which is also known as 'Surrey', is ideal back-up for a garden in which miniatures are grown as the blooms are carried in good clusters of rosette-type blooms. It is good enough to win numerous international awards. (Kordes)

Sonnenkind
One of several miniatures that were produced in the late 1980s by Kordes in Germany. It is a really bright yellow with good cutting form and fine growth. (Kordes)

97

Starglo
The touch of red on the petal edge gives this 1973 rose a fresh look, and it is equally good when in bud or in open bloom. Watch it for blackspot though.

Starla
This good double white has just a hint of gold at its heart. It is a vigorous grower. (Sheila Lee)

98

Stars 'n' Stripes

'Stars 'n' Stripes' was the first of the man-hybridized striped roses. Before this, any stripes we had came from mutations, but here Ralph Moore produced a fine, colourful and even patriotic little rose that helped other breeders get their start. It is a bushy enough grower to make a good, small hedge.

Stolen Moment

Ten petals that begin in a tightly closed bud that is beauty in itself but opens to a lovely light mauve flower on a vigorous bush.

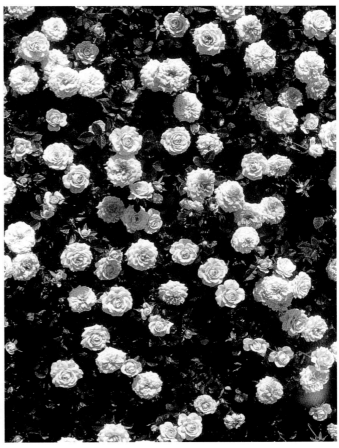

Sunblaze

When the French firm of Meilland took the group name 'Sunblaze' for its collection of miniature roses it was certainly on to a winner. The roses, mostly hybridized in their own famous centre in Antibes, cover the whole spectrum of the colour range, and they offer rose lovers in Europe a totally different concept of miniatures, a concept that was soon picked up worldwide, and now there are few countries in the world where there are not some of the 'Sunblaze' roses. All the plants grow on their roots and are as pretty, tough and disease resistant as you can get. They also have the happy disposition of always being in flower. In addition, they make ideal container plants for conservatory or short indoor use before being planted out in the garden. On a purely personal basis I find that 'Lady Sunblaze', 'Yellow Sunblaze' and 'Pink Sunblaze' are high on my list of desirable garden plants. (E. Ulzaga, courtesy Meilland & Cie)

Apricot Sunblaze

Lady Sunblaze

Pink Sunblaze

Orange Sunblaze

Yellow Sunblaze

Yorkshire Sunblaze

103

Swansong
The white blooms are – sometimes – almost perfect. But for all my own pleasure in it, 'Swansong' has been rated 'stingy', yet still won Queen of the Show awards. Needs extra care and attention to make it grow really well.

Sweet Chariot
The ruffled purple flowers are quick to repeat, and this is a marvellous variety for hanging baskets or rockeries or as part of larger group planting. It is also very fragrant. The flowers have the appealing habit of having all shades of mauve, lavender and lilac at the same time.

Tara Allison
A lively, orange-red variety
with some silver on the reverse
of a whole host of informal
blooms, 'Tara Allison' is
healthy and hardy. It was
named for the daughter of June
and Jerry Justice, the Oregon
growers.

Teddy Bear
The colour is officially classified
as red, although it seems to me
to be nearer to terracotta. It is a
new and promising rose,
especially suitable for those
who like flower arranging.

Timothy Berlen
Everyone talks about the
vibrancy of the colour of
'Timothy Berlen', which is
officially an orange blend. The
bloom is a little big for some,
but most gardeners delight in
the good form.

Warm Welcome

This climbing miniature caused one of the sensations of 1988 when it just about swept the board by winning the Royal National Rose Society's top awards in Britain. The surprise was not occasioned by the variety, which had been glowingly commented upon for the three years it was under trial, but because it was a climber, and climbers do not normally win big awards, and also because it was bred by an amateur, Chris Warner, and amateurs do not normally win with that sort of emphasis.

Why Not

Ralph Moore says that he was wondering whether he should introduce this bright-eyed single, when one of his staff said positively 'Why not!' So, with its vigorous growth and sunny complexion, it went on to become a winner. The blooms are long lasting. (Sheila Lee)

Winsome

The super mauve flowers are borne on a tallish gangling bush. Some say that it is too big for the miniatures, but it is too small to be anything else, so it certainly deserves recognition. The flowers, almost lilac in colour, have a lovely, double form, with petals of a good substance. (Sheila Lee)

Wit's End

I took a plant of 'Wit's End' to photograph and found that the original had a mutation, or sport, growing in it. This happens with many varieties, and in this case the lighter coloured sport, which can also be seen here, has a lot going for it. It is now being propagated and might even be on the market one day. There is a lesson here for all gardeners: watch out for plants that may have a different flower on them – they could be even better than the original.

Work of Art
This climber has well-shaped blooms in a blend of orange and yellow. It flowers continuously and has lots of good foliage. It is good enough to reach 6 ft (1.8 m) high.

Yellow Doll
Although this is an old rose, it is still good enough to appear in many catalogues. It loses out to more modern yellows, however, in the flower shape, which at best could be called 'informal'.

Zwergenfee
This is one of the many miniatures introduced by Germany's great hybridizer, Kordes. It is larger than normal, but it is compact and busy and makes a very good bedding miniature. The flowers are orange-red. (Kordes)

Zwergkönigin

'Zwergkönigin' is also known as 'Dwarf Queen '81'. The year is important as there was another rose of the same name in the 1950s, but here is a case of good replacement. This deep pink variety does grow taller than most miniatures, but it has neat, bushy growth and is a wonderful producer of long-stemmed, beautifully shaped blooms. (Kordes) topped with soil taken from another part of the garden. The coverings can be held in place with chicken wire or netting or with loose branches of fir trees that will keep their foliage. If you are caught unawares by really cold, drying winds or freezing, an old blanket staked into the ground over the bushes can do the trick, but this should be used as a temporary cover only. The same goes for an upturned bucket weighted down with a brick to keep it from blowing away.

The most effective covers are those made from organic materials that are mounded up around the bush. These provide moisture and protection and can be left on until the danger of heavy frosts has passed. If you have problems with covering materials being blown away, there is a fibre glass, rose winterizer mesh material that is widely advertised in rose magazines. When it is placed around the rose, the mesh is wide enough to permit drainage but tight enough to hold in the leaves, peat moss or other material that might be easily disturbed. Early uncovering will not hasten growth but might be the real problem in survival. Leave the covering on as long as possible, then take out the garden hose on a fine, warm day and wash it away. You will often be surprised at the amount of growth that has begun underneath.

Nothing is perfect, of course, and the weight of organic materials can cause some stems to break. In addition, if the weather does not get cold enough, plants can rot underneath the covering. The cleaning-up process is not as easy as it is often made out to be, either, and straw in particular is very hard to clean away in the spring.

If you use leaves, beware the damage they can cause as they mass together over the plants. One way of avoiding the problem is to put a plastic covering over the bush and then add the leaves around it, before covering it all with the mesh material. This may seem an expensive method, but many liquids, arrive in large plastic containers, and particularly useful are the 1 gallon (4.5 litre) milk containers or the large soft drink bottles. Simply cut the bottoms off these and place them over the bush. When spring comes, it just means clearing the leaves away to use as a mulch later and leaving the cover on the plant until you are absolutely sure that the weather is going to stay good. The temporary cover on the bushes will bring them into growth far quicker than a plant left out to grow its own way.

One further problem with winter protection is that rodents can decide to make the little mound their home for the winter, and they will eat away at the plants until there is nothing left. The only thing to do here is to lay some bait down and hope that it will clear away any troublesome visitors. Do remember, however, that the bait can be as deadly to a human or another animal as to a rodent. You can always buy another rose bush.

All this advice relates to bushes of miniature roses. The real problems come with tree or standard roses, which are far more susceptible to periods of frost–thaw–frost because they stand so high. If conditions warrant it, standards should be lifted and buried in the ground. I have seen some Styrofoam upright, coffin-like covers made for these as well, and there is the old-fashioned method of covering the whole tree with straw and then tying it on with a piece of old sacking or a blanket. The important part of these roses is the crown, which must be well covered with a material that will keep it both moist and safe from freezing. If you live in an area that suffers from cold winters, the simplest way to grow standard or tree roses is to plant them in large pots. Whether these are stood on the patio or sunk in the garden, they need only be moved to an unheated shed, cellar or garage to overwinter in safety.

5

PESTS AND DISEASES

If you were to make a full list of the pests and diseases that can appear in the garden, you would probably sell it to the top bidder and take off to a high-rise with not a leaf in sight. That's the bad news. The good news is that no one meets all the baddies all the time, and the miniature rose is resilient enough to win most wars as long as it has a little help.

It is easy to panic if you don't know how to treat the bugs and predators that arrive in the garden, but the truth is that most attacks by insects and diseases are episodic, and with a little bit of commonsense all can be put right in a matter of a few days.

Pests

There is no doubt that if a garden is neglected or not properly cared for it can become home to a plague. I believe in combating pests as early as possible, and certainly before they reach plague proportions. I have experimented with soapy water, but although it washes the little critters off the stems, they just lie doggo for a few minutes to make me think they are dead and then begin to climb a new stem, breeding as they go. However, recently introduced natural organic formulations that use soaps as a base have proved most effective, and researchers have managed to isolate the most effective fatty acids, which, when blended with some synthetic products, give the full benefit of natural organics. These do work against all aphids, mites and scale insects in the rose garden.

The phrase 'integrated pest management' is frequently heard these days. This is just another way of saying that we should be sensible about the use of inorganic sprays, but it does offer alternatives to

spraying, including the use of natural predators such as the ladybird (ladybug) to take care of aphids. However, if the pest problem does get beyond you, many gardeners will say that the only thing to do is spray with a systemic insecticide. This will get into the plant and take care of the present generation of pests as well as those that have still to arrive. However, more and more people are choosing not to use systemic sprays in their gardens because they are environmentally unfriendly. Most of these sprays are highly toxic, and when you use them you must take special precautions for your own and your neighbours' safety (as described later in this chapter). Ask yourself if it is worth it. You will then probably join the growing band of those who are more concerned about the health of the world than about the health of a plant and begin to look around for alternative control methods.

One of the high-tech solutions to pest control that is being investigated at present is said to be triggered by light and to kill insects within seconds. The spray contains an amino acid, known as ALA, which is combined with a chemical modulator that causes an immediate reaction when it is exposed to sunlight. It is said to be totally safe to humans, and there is no way that the bugs can develop an immunity to it. Among other ideas also being investigated, but not likely to become generally accepted for several years, will be the wider use of pheromones – odours that are attractive to insects – while the use of sticky traps to catch insects will also be seen more often. Scientists now also believe that gardens should be landscaped so that they will not attract or shelter pests. This means placing plants away from areas in which pests may breed and thrive.

No doubt other pesticides that leave no toxic residue will become standard for use in the garden, but if these are not available yet there is no need to panic; the list of predators that follows may seem frightening, but I have never seen them all together, and very few gardeners ever have either.

Aphids

Most people call aphids greenfly whether they are brown, orange, reddish or black. Whatever their colour, all do the same damage, which is to take the vigour away from the plant. If you are not squeamish, a finger-and-thumb round of your garden will go a long way towards keeping the plague at bay. Numerous contact sprays are available, some of which are inorganic (chemical) while others are natural organics (that is, they are obtained from plant and animal sources). Contact sprays must be repeated as soon as you see new pests arrive. This advice also applies to all the other pests that follow. You can get some biological control with ladybirds (ladybugs), but I have found that as soon as the aphids vanish so, too, do the predators, which generally fail to reappear with the aphids' return.

Spider Mite

The real curse of miniature roses, especially in hot and dry conditions, is the spider mite. It is a small sucking insect, which is generally found on the underside of leaves and which is difficult to get rid of once it settles in. It is so small – about a quarter of the size of a pinhead – that you will need good eyesight or help from a magnifying glass to spot it. It stunts growth and discolours leaves until they become brittle and fall off. The first sign of an attack may be the arrival of small 'webs' (similar to tiny spider webs but slightly more dense) on the growing shoots of roses or even around pots. Infestation can be checked by aiming a fine jet of water under the foliage, but this must be consistent, and it is not easy to spray under the foliage of any plant, let alone that of a miniature rose. There are specific sprays available, but the mite tends to build up an immunity to them, so they should be varied from time to time. Of all the pests to which miniature roses are prone, this is the hardest to

combat, and it can reach plague proportions very quickly, especially if you grow your miniatures under glass. Biological controls are being investigated, and it is hoped that a suitable predator will be found. (See also p. 27.)

Froghopper

The white, spittle-like froth, better known as cuckoo-spit, that is seen in leaf joints and around buds harbours a small, yellowish insect, the froghopper. As the froghopper matures it can damage foliage and leaves. Give the affected parts of the bush a really strong spray of water to wash away the spittle and expose the bug, which can be easily picked off.

Rose Scale

These small, whitish insects mostly infest older wood. Use a good, strong dose of one of the organic insecticides.

Caterpillars

You will know if caterpillars are about by the irregular shaped holes in the leaves. If you do not want the trouble of hand-picking them, use one of the specific insecticides.

Leaf-rolling Sawfly

The larvae of this particular sawfly hide away in leaves, which roll tightly around them to protect them. Pick off the affected leaves and squeeze them between your forefinger and thumb to kill the greyish-green grubs. You may find that infestation is more common if roses are grown under trees.

Leafhopper

You may have seen these pale yellow, hopping insects when you brought flowers into the house from the garden. If you look for their homes on the foliage, you will spot some pale, mottled patches. After a bad attack the foliage will often fall off.

Beetles

These make holes in foliage similar to those made by caterpillars, but if you see a brownish beetle among the leaves, you will know you have the may-bug or cockchafer. Pick them off and destroy them. Various other beetles can be found among roses, but few of them bother with miniatures because the blooms are too small for them to bother about. This is, fortunately, true of the Japanese beetle, which is a real scourge in parts of the United States, especially on larger roses. There are traps and some sprays available, but keeping a daily watch on the blooms and disposing of the first arrivals will be effective. There is a bacteriological spray that can be used against the beetles, but this is unlikely to work unless you have the cooperation of your neighbours, whose gardens may well be where the beetles are also breeding.

Vine Weevil

The vine weevil lays its eggs in and around the roots of potted miniatures, and the cream-coloured, motionless larvae eventually feed on the roots and can very quickly kill even a full-sized plant. A bio-degradeable bait was recently announced, and it is said to be deadly to the vine weevil. It is laid deeply between layers of dry leaves and does not, therefore, harm birds or other creatures. Indeed, the developer of the product, a retired English farmer, demonstrated the harmless nature of the bait by eating some himself. He is keeping its formula, which is also effective against slugs, secret.

Slugs and Snails

As far as roses are concerned, slugs and snails are fairly harmless creatures, but they do gather where there is plenty of moisture and feed on decaying organic matter. If they seem to be causing problems, put some beer in a tin or saucer and sink it in the ground. Both slugs and snails are attracted to the moisture and the scent and topple in. If you decide to use slug bait make a small tent with plastic and lay the bait evenly inside. Make an entrance only big enough for the snails to get in to prevent birds pecking at the bait. You may also find tortrix moths and leaf miners but specific insecticides are available for both.

Diseases

Three main diseases – blackspot, mildew and rust may affect your miniatures.

Blackspot

This disease is just what the name implies – black spots, roughly circular in shape, with a ragged edge,

are seen on the leaves. They turn yellow, and, when they have completely taken over a leaf, it falls off the bush. No matter what you may be told, no hybrid rose is totally immune to the disease, although some are more resistant than others. The best means of control is to have a clean garden. Never allow leaves with the disease to fall on the ground or to overwinter, and pick off foliage at the first sign of infection.

Mildew

You will know if your roses have mildew by the appearance of a white fungus on the leaves, stems and even the flowers. In extreme cases it can actually warp the stems. A century ago mildew was the greatest scourge of the rose garden, and the recommended treatment was to cover the finger and thumb with sulphur and then wipe each affected leaf from top to bottom. Sulphur can, of course, also be used as a spray, which will be even more effective if a little washing-up liquid is added to act as a spreader. Many gardeners use a sulphur spray during the dormant season, when it will also have some effect on scale insects and insect eggs, although its most important function is to kill any overwintering fungal spores. Today trials are well under way to find natural methods of combating garden diseases, and one experiment with a yeast extract has already shown promising results with wheat, maize and barley, and it may be used against mildew in roses. The extract encourages the plant to fight the disease itself and, in the process, also improves yields. Until this and other organic alternatives are commercially available, however, mildew can be kept at bay by siting rose bushes so that they are not growing in a 'mildew trap' – that is, in a spot where their roots will dry out and there is no movement of air around the plants – and by ensuring that they are kept well supplied with food and water.

Rust

A hundred years ago rust was not considered to be as troublesome as mildew, but today the opposite is true. You will know if your roses are infected by the appearance of small orange spots on the foliage. The damage is really done on the undersides of the leaves, which, if they are left alone, will eventually become covered with an orange and black deposit that falls on other leaves and on to the ground. Remove infected foliage immediately and use a spray to keep the disease under control. There is one product that can be used as both a cure and protection, but it is not yet available to most home gardeners. It is also hoped that a natural method of control and cure will be found as research is carried out into the way the spores that carry the disease function.

Spraying

After years and years of trying out different techniques, ranging from constant spraying to total neglect, I can tell you that neglect always leads to problems. The strong, well-tended rose will always be able to perform better than a weak, neglected plant in the battle against diseases and be better able to withstand the attacks of garden pests, but there is absolutely nothing a rose can do to combat these ills if it is left to its own devices.

There are three schools of thought about using sprays to combat diseases and pests. Some people say that you should not spray until you see the first black spot or the first aphid. A second group believes in the value of the old boy scout motto – be prepared – and sprays as a means of prevention rather than cure. The third group, which is growing steadily, does not believe in using sprays of any kind whatsoever. I belong to the second group, although I do have sympathy with the third.

I am often told that, because I follow the 'be prepared' school, I will use far more chemicals in my garden in one year than the gardener who waits to see what is going to happen before taking action. I absolutely refute that charge, and I base my argument on scientific experiments that have shown that it takes about six weeks for a blackspot spore that lands on a rose leaf to develop and form a spot that is approximately 1 in (2.5 cm) across. If you wait for that spot to develop, it is going to take you another five weeks to eradicate it with double-strength, weekly sprayings, and during that time the spores will have spread around the rest of the garden and become a major problem. If, however, you have taken preventative action, you are likely to have eliminated the original spore before it got the chance to form a large colony and, thereafter fortnightly sprays of a normal strength fungicide will be all that is necessary.

My advice to everyone who wants to grow disease-free roses is to feed them well and to spray them regularly from the moment the first leaves appear. One year, in part of my garden that is not seen by the public, I left six bushes untouched until the first signs of blackspot and mildew appeared. These bushes were a total disaster, and even weekly sprays did not clear them of disease until long after the first flush of blooms was over.

As far as pests are concerned, however, it is possible to adopt the 'don't spray until you see it' policy. As soon as you see an aphid or any other harmful insect, you should take action, but even then I prefer the finger-and-thumb method, using an insecticidal spray only as a last resort.

No matter how big or small your garden or what method of control you decide upon, the message has to be 'begin early'. First, clear away any old leaves that may be lying around the garden; they may well be infected. This applies to dried material, too, because fungal spores can survive for a long time, even in severe winters. As soon as the foliage begins to appear, start your control programme and keep it going right to the end of the season. Over the years I have tried many experiments and have come to the conclusion that roses sprayed with a fungicide immediately after pruning and regularly every two weeks throughout the season will be kept totally clear of most diseases, although rust may rear its head in midsummer.

What every gardener wants is a system of spraying that will keep diseases under control, that will not harm the environment and that will not cost an arm and a leg. The one great thing about miniature roses is that, because of their size, you will not need nearly as much spray as you would for larger roses. When you do spray, make sure that all the foliage on each plant is covered, and this includes the undersides of leaves. Part spraying will only treat part of the problem. Try to avoid buying more fungicide or pesticide than you will use in a season, although buying a large container does work out less expensive than having to purchase two or three smaller packs. However, do remember that despite the long shelf-life of most spray materials, the fresh product is always best.

There are a number of important rules to remember when it comes to the actual job of spraying.

- Read the manufacturer's instructions carefully before you begin to use the spray and have them in front of you as you mix. Follow the instruction to the letter.
- Do not mix more than you expect to use at one time and never store diluted spray in bottles. There have been fatal accidents when even highly educated gardeners mistook spray for lemonade.
- Take extreme care with all material, no matter how low the toxicity levels.
- Use a good spray tank, and an adjustable nozzle that gives a fine stream of spray.
- Water all roses thoroughly the day before you spray to supply moisture to the plants so that they do not have to rely on the liquid content of the spray. If the plants are dry, some of the foliage may show unsightly burn marks.
- Forget what the neighbours may say or what is the current fashion and wear rubber gloves, a face mask and a hat, and make sure your arms and legs are covered.
- Mix the spray in a well-ventilated area. Do not mix or use a spray on a windy day when the drift might fall on you, on your neighbours' gardens or on other plants in your own garden that will not appreciate it.
- Fill the spray tank with the required amount of water and then add the spray powder or liquid. If you put the spray material in first it could stay at the bottom of the tank and not dilute to the correct solution.
- Never spray in strong sunshine.
- Wet all bushes until they begin to drip.
- Do not spray when it is raining or when it looks as if it is likely to rain. All sprays need to stay on the foliage for at least two hours to be effective.
- Continue to spray against the main diseases right through to late autumn. Too often gardeners stop at the end of summer and, as it only takes blackspot a couple of weeks to become established, bushes are then defoliated just when the fine autumn flowering is at its height.

6

PROPAGATION

Miniature roses are propagated in three main ways – by budding, by grafting or by taking cuttings. For the rose grower who wants to try something different in propagation, it is also possible to root them by layering, while a horticultural chemist in laboratory conditions might try micropropagation. If I had to use one method of reproduction, I would immediately opt for cuttings. Modern miniature roses give the lie to the old belief that roses are hard to root from cuttings, and indeed, most of them root with an ease that is beaten (marginally) only by the geranium or fuchsia. Moreover, if a new modern miniature does not grow easily from cuttings, it will not find a place with the growers who need easily propagated varieties. Today there are dozens of small nurseries throughout the world, and especially in the United States, whose success is due to their ability to grow roses successfully on their own roots.

The important thing to remember is that you can propagate as many plants as you like for your own use, but if you dare to sell them you could be found to be in breach of the patent laws. Practically every new rose is patented, and this legal protection lasts for many years.

Cuttings

Growing new plants from cuttings is simple. The whole process begins with a piece of rose wood about 5 in (13 cm) long, that has carried a flower. It does not matter what time of year you take this wood, although you will have more success in spring and mid-autumn than in the strong heat of midsummer, when it can take twice as long to root a cutting. There should be

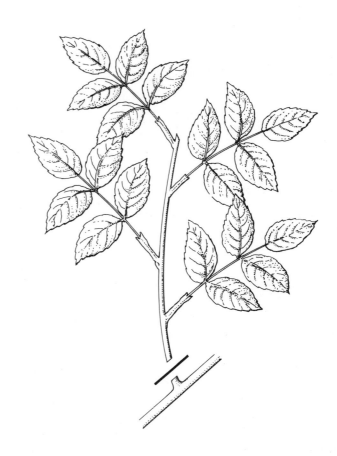

Cut a piece of rose wood about 5 in (13 cm) long with four sets of leaflets along the stem.

four sets of leaflets along the stem. Snip off the spent bloom at the top and trim the wood down to the first set of leaflets. At the base, trim off the bottom two sets of leaflets and leave the other two on, although it does

Having removed the flower head and cut back to the first set of
leaflets, then remove the bottom two sets of leaflets, as shown,
and trim the base of the stem diagonally, just below the
bottom leaf axil.

help to pinch these to two leaves each or to cut off part
of each leaf. Trim the base of the cutting diagonally,
just below the bottom leaf axil. Sturdy little cuttings
will produce a better plant more quickly than twiggy
ones.

While you are preparing the planting mixture
stand the cutting in some off-cold water to which can
be added a drop of vitamin B-1, if you are feeling
extravagant, or some seaweed solution; although either
of these will help the cutting get over the shock more
quickly and leave it ready to root, they are not really
necessary. Fill the container, which can be anything
that has some drainage holes – a small plastic plant
pot, a peat pot or even a polystyrene foam cup with
holes punched in the base, for example – with a
moistened seed or cutting mixture. Make a suitable
hole to take the cutting, which should be dipped into a
hormone rooting medium before being placed in

Dip the cutting into a hormone rooting powder and insert it in
the pot.

the pot. Firm it in with your fingers. The two sets of leaves should be above the soil level, and the two leaf axils from which the foliage has been removed should be below it. If you have more than one cutting, place them around the edge of the container, although do not put more than three cuttings in one pot. Water well, then slip the pot into a plastic bag and carefully insert some twigs or a bent wire coat-hanger to prevent the plastic touching the cuttings. Tie the top of the bag with a wire twist and place it where it will get dappled sunshine. The rooting process will take about six weeks, and often a great deal less.

You have to make sure that the cutting is kept in a warm, humid environment. You can place it under a growing rose bush (or any other plant for that matter) where the sunshine can be filtered through the leaves, but do make sure that it is in a sunny spot. You can put it on a window-sill, but make sure it is out of direct sunlight. I know one rosarian who roots all his cuttings in small pots, covers them with plastic bags and leaves them hanging from the lower branches of an apple tree. When the new leaflets are growing well the bag can be opened and the plant gradually hardened off before being repotted or planted out. This sort of small cutting makes an ideal rockery or container plant.

It is also possible to plant the cuttings directly into the garden. Prepare the stem in the way described above, make a hole in the soil and fill it with the seed or cutting compost and then plant the cutting. Firm it in, water it well and cover it with a large glass jar. When it looks as though it is growing well, remove the jar and the little plant can get on with its new life.

Wherever you grow your cuttings, however, do not be too impatient to see how they are doing. Leave them alone unless it seems that they may be drying out, when you can simply open the plastic bag or lift the jar and water them.

If you plan to increase your roses by taking large numbers of cuttings, you will have to provide either a greenhouse or some protective covering unless you live in an area of high sunshine. In my own small greenhouse I simply take a cutting and place it at the base of an already-growing rose. There is no ceremony about it – the cutting often goes in without the benefit of a rooting agent or vitamin help – and I have enjoyed an astonishing success rate because the con-

ditions I provide for growing roses in the greenhouse are all that are needed to make the cuttings respond. The problem with this method is that the rooted plantlets have to be taken from the soil, which can so disturb their root systems that they die. An alternative method is to use a soil-less pot for the cutting so that the rooted plant can be taken out from the larger pot without any root disturbance.

The ideal way to grow a number of cuttings is to plant them in a mist propagator in a soil-less medium made up of vermiculite, perlite and peat. Here, under controlled conditions, they will root more quickly and the percentage of successful plants will greatly increase; some growers, in fact, claim 100 per cent success by this method. The same conditions must exist as for the cuttings grown in a plastic bag – warmth, moisture and light.

Layering
A few years ago I said that layering miniature roses was not a practicable proposition. Since then, however, a number of new types of miniatures roses have appeared on the market. These are lax growers, which are mainly the ground-cover types, and they can be successfully layered during the growing season.

The advantage of layering a ground-cover rose is that it is growing exactly how you need it – close to the ground. Make an incision in the lower side of a branch so that the cut stays open when the soil is around it. The wound you make should produce roots, not heal, so you have to hold it open in some way – you can wedge a small stone or sliver of wood in the incision. Cover the wound with soil and hold the branch in place with some strong wire or a large stone. Leave the branch undisturbed until the autumn when it should have produced roots and be ready for separation from the parent plant. Layering is a simple way of increasing plants such as 'Nozomi', 'Snow Carpet', 'Angelita', 'Arctic Sunrise', 'Sweet Chariot' and 'Suma', or any roses that tend to be of a weeping type.

Budding
What bothers many people who grow their roses from cuttings is that it takes a couple of summers for the plant to reach the same stage of development that budded or grafted roses have reached at the time they are bought. It is generally forgotten that the budded

plant has taken all of two years in time-consuming, field-growing conditions to reach this stage, and that budding is a technique that does take a little skill to perfect.

My own method, which I must admit I now use very rarely because I find cuttings much more acceptable, is to pot up some rootstocks, which are available from most professional nurserymen. Budding must be done in summer. The shoot from which the bud is taken should have a half-open flower. Do not confuse this process with a bud bloom; in this case a bud is the little eye inside the leaf axil. Select the bud from halfway down the stem and cut the stem so that the bud is about $\frac{1}{2}$ in (13 mm) above the bottom cut. Strip off all foliage and thorns and make a small cut about $\frac{1}{2}$ in (13 mm) above the eye to be used and steadily pull away the bark. You will be left with the shield that holds the eye, and this is what you will use as the main bud.

Make a T-shaped cut in the selected rootstock at soil level, open the bark and slide the new bud in. Tie this in place with a small piece of plastic or some raffia. The following spring the bud should have swollen and be ready to burst into a new tree. Trim the plant back to just above the bud and, if the tie or rubber band is still in place, remove it carefully. The plant will flower that summer but must not be moved until the following autumn when it will have matured. If you have difficulty getting rootstock on which to do the budding, root any cutting from a rampant climber or rambler or even from a wild hedgerow rose.

If you are interested in budding some plants, it would be as well to have someone demonstrate the method to you. It is actually simpler to do than to describe. You should also practise on some wood, because the most important part is successfully prising the shield and the bud away from the old wood. These days, however, budding is best left to professionals.

Micropropagation

This is proving a very successful way of propagating many, but not all, miniature roses; some roses grown by this method fail to reproduce the same sort of bush as the parent, often growing too tall, too low or carrying fewer blooms or blooms that take on a different shading. No doubt as the process, which involves impregnating the tissue in a chemical solution, is improved, most roses will be grown by this method. It is far more commercially oriented than any other method as up to 10,000 roses can be grown from one bush in a year. That is a phenomenal rate of increase when you consider that in the first year of a new variety only three or four bushes might be obtained; it would take five years of budding to achieve a total of 10,000 new plants. The method is already being used extensively in Europe, where miniature roses roll out of the laboratory by the million, are hardened off and can be brought into flower right through the year, even in time for the lucrative Christmas market. No doubt it will be tomorrow's method for growing roses, but until then it is best left to the professionals, and the ordinary gardener could do a lot worse than to take a few cuttings and propagage the plants for personal use.

7

*H*YBRIDIZING

If you really want to try for a moment of glory in the world of the miniature rose, start hybridizing now. Hybridizing is the technical plant term for breeding, and if one activity in the rose world will be remembered in a hundred years, it will be the number of amateur hybridizers who enjoyed success in the last decades of the twentieth century. The amateur breeder has turned the rose world upside down and has had an exceptionally exciting impact on the world of miniature rose breeding. The number of new miniature rose varieties has risen from a mere handful into the hundreds, with million-dollar firms being established on the strength of this output.

It would, however, be wrong to think that the modern breeding of little roses is all big business. It is anything but that. In the United States, where the boom in miniature rose breeding began, most of today's biggest growers began as mere amateurs, and those professional businesses with generations of breeders behind them have raced in to get in on the act. For all that, few of the professional firms have yet to achieve anything near the perfection or the output of those who started as amateurs.

My own introduction to hybridizing came about one day when I arrived home from work to find my eldest son busily taking pollen from 'Crimson Glory' and putting it on 'Piccadilly', both hybrid tea roses. He told me that as I had been talking about doing some hybridizing for years he thought he would give me a shove in the right direction. That shove turned into a downhill roll, and I began to hybridize roses. I turned from large roses to miniatures when it became too big an operation for my greenhouse, which is only

12×8 ft (3.7×2.4 m). It was not that miniature roses presented a greater challenge, it was just that they are easier to work with in terms of space. Where I could have only six or seven large roses, I can work with as many as twenty smaller ones.

The wonderful thing about hybridizing is that you need only two rose bushes to begin with, and from them you could finish up with a few hundred seeds by the end of the year, which, by the following summer, might well have produced a winning rose.

The best way to hybridize miniatures is to have two different varieties that come into bloom at the same time growing in pots. You will need some cover for the operation unless you live in a warm, dry part of the world – southern California is ideal – but don't be deterred by a lack of facilities. One top breeder, John Sheridan, who lives in Catford, London, grows his roses on the kitchen window-sill and has had a couple of international successes.

There are no rules governing the roses that you use, but the best advice is 'breed from the best to the best and hope for the best'. This is what horse breeders tell each other, and it is a rule that is repeated in the plant world. Before you begin, however, look around for at least one variety that is known to set seeds. You can often find this out by looking at the parentage of the roses that are in commerce, or you can make a note of the miniatures in your own garden that set hips easily. Remember, though, that roses that set seeds do not always set seeds that germinate. Among the top miniatures that have been used in breeding in recent years you will find 'Rise 'n' Shine', 'Sheri Anne', 'Anytime', 'Yellow Jewel', 'Golden

Angel', 'Pink Petticoat', 'Libby', 'Fire Princess' and 'Black Jade'. It is a matter of trial and error. Some years ago I used 'Loving Touch' for a whole season and then was told that none of the seeds would germinate. My advisers were not totally right, but they weren't totally wrong – I had spotty germination, but it was still over 25 per cent, which is quite good. In the same year I had almost 100 per cent germination with seeds from 'Rise 'n' Shine'. Once you find a plant that gives you good germination keep it in good condition with lots of attention, because it often happens that two plants of the same variety will fail to give equally good germination or seed set. I recently used a couple of plants of a seedling of my own, 'Kiss 'n' Tell', and found that one plant set seeds every time and the other, even though I used the same pollen, did not.

As with all things, hybridizing becomes easier with experience, but here are the stages for breeding your own miniature roses.

Select a rose that is just beginning to open and carefully remove all the petals and all the anthers. After about 24 hours the pollen from the father plant can be transferred to the stigma of the first (mother) rose. Remember to attach a label saying which roses you have crossed.

- When the flowers are at the quarter-open stage, gently remove all the petals, making sure you do not leave any little bits behind. Use either a small pair of scissors or tweezers to remove all the anthers, and if you are using this pollen for crossing on to another rose, save it on a sheet of paper and mark the name at the top.
- Prepare a second rose, which may also be used as a mother (seed producer) or father (pollen) parent, in the same way.
- Do not mix the pollen, but place the separate sheets of paper in a fridge overnight. Pollen can also be stored in baby-food jars, but they must be absolutely dry. If it is stored in an airtight jar, pollen will keep for up to two weeks in normal house temperatures; it will keep for much longer in a fridge, but it will need a day or two to regenerate itself when you take it out.
- The pollen, whether on paper or in a jar, should be ready by the next day. If you gently shake the anthers and you see the deposit of yellow pollen you will know it is ready.
- Use your index finger or a small brush to transfer the pollen from the first rose to the stigma of the second rose. And vice versa. Attach a small tag to the flower to tell you which roses you have crossed.
- If the cross-pollination takes place in a greenhouse there is no need to cover the rose, but if you do it in the open you will need to place a small paper cover over the rose head.
- As other blooms begin to flower, continue with the same method, but it may be possible to obtain pollen from other roses elsewhere. It is great fun to experiment, and using the pollen of large roses, old roses and even climbing roses on miniatures often brings success. There is no end to the experiments that you can carry out.

That is the end of the actual hybridizing process. Now it is just a matter of waiting for the pods to swell and the seeds to grow. Leave the pods on the bush for 12–14 weeks, in which time they should turn orange and be ready for harvesting. Some varieties will not actually go orange, but will be ready when they are a darkish grey. There are several different ways of working with the seed, but the most widely used system is to take each hip, and open it individually. Give the seeds the water test – that is, put them in a cupful of water and throw away the floaters, for only those that sink are fertile. Wrap these seeds in a small piece of damp paper towel, place them inside a small plastic bag and put them away in the bottom of the fridge, remembering to label them clearly with the name of the cross. Leave them in the vegetable compartment of the refrigerator for about six weeks. This is as simple a scheme as any, although the best germination I ever had was one year when I put all the seeds in their coverings in a glass jar standing on the kitchen window-sill. I left them for six weeks, never allowing them to dry out, and when I opened the papers up, many of the seeds had already germinated.

Whichever system you select, the next step is to plant the seeds in ordinary seed trays. Use a recognized seed potting mix, into which some growers mix a little perlite to stop the soil compacting too closely around the seeds. Even the famous have problems with this; Ralph Moore told me that one year he lost 90 per cent of his seedlings because the soil mix was wrong. Place the seeds about $\frac{1}{2}$ in (13 mm) under the soil and about 1 in (2.5 cm) apart. Keep the soil watered; if the rose seeds dry out at all you have been wasting your time. I place my trays on the greenhouse bench and leave them there without a cover, although this is not advisable for anyone who might have mice, which will open every single seed to get the embryo of the plant for food. If mice are a problem, cover the seeds with some plastic or, better still, a sheet of glass, but do make sure that it is wiped clear of moisture; otherwise there might be too much condensation.

In a matter of weeks the first seeds should be showing through. Two little leaves like rabbit's ears appear first, and are eventually followed by the rose leaves. I have found that seeds planted in January will be in flower in March, April and May. If the seed trays are deep enough – those 9 in (23 cm) deep are hard to find but are ideal – the plants can be left to flower. If the trays are the normal 2–3 in (5–7.5 cm) deep, the seedlings should be lifted as soon as the first two leaves have been established and placed in small pots with a good potting mixture. Always lift them by the leaves, as the slightest pressure can damage the tiny stem growth. This is personal advice, although I have seen Ralph Moore grow all his seedlings until their second flowering in trays 2 in (5 cm) deep.

Now you have your own miniature roses and all you have to do is wait and see how good they are. Give them time to see how they develop. Do not throw them away until you are sure there is no hope for them, because even the most unpromising roses are beautiful in their own ways.

If you want to transfer a growing plant (as opposed to a very new seedling) from the seed tray to keep it, place it in a mist tray with heat and constant misting for a week or so. Grow it on for a year or two before you make a decision about keeping it. Do not try to take cuttings from a small plant or you may lose it. In its second summer it should be strong enough to be propagated. It may not put you in the same league as the masters, but who cares, this is a personal moment of glory!

8

EXHIBITING

Winning is fun! And once you have won at a rose show it seems that you are hooked for all time. I know this from my own experience, and in recent years I have had the additional excitement of watching roses that I have hybridized winning prizes for other gardeners.

The art of exhibiting brings together all the other techniques of the garden – the growing, the caring and the sharing of roses – and it extends the pleasure far beyond that of many other hobbies. The way shows are organized may vary from country to country, but they all have the same intention – the search for perfection. A perfect bloom in Akron, Ohio, is also a perfect bloom in Otago, New Zealand.

Miniatures have broadened the whole scope of exhibiting and could well be the saviours of rose shows throughout the world. This is because they are easier to grow than large roses and, more importantly, are easier to transport. Packed in a picnic box with dry ice, they can travel for days and still retain their beauty and freshness. Exhibitors of miniatures travel hundreds of miles to show their blooms, and among the visitors to the Royal National Rose Society's Summer Festival of Roses in 1990 was Dr Tommy Cairns who had travelled thousands of miles with his roses all the way from southern California. He could well be the first of many to travel so far as the transportation of the little roses becomes easier and easier.

There are no secrets to winning consistently at shows, and if you follow the cultivation methods that I have described you will be well on the way to being a winner. If you want to go one better then I suggest that you might consider giving the bushes a liquid feed (one high in phosphorus) on a regular basis, and even as late as two weeks before the show.

For a weekend show you can begin to cut blooms as early as the previous Wednesday. Once you have cut the blooms that are ready, give the bed or other planting place a good soaking to help the other blooms to move a little faster. Cut all blooms a little longer than you think will be necessary, always remembering that they need at least two sets of leaves (if possible) on a stem. By cutting the stem longer than needed initially, you will be able to re-cut it under water, which will help prevent the blooms going limp. Do make sure that they are placed in water immediately after cutting. Ordinary water with a few drops of lemon or another citrus juice will be good enough, but carbonated water (made from one part of any bubbly drink like 7-Up or Mountain Dew to two parts of tap water) also seems to be effective. If your blooms do go limp, hold the stems in very hot water for a few seconds and they will begin to perk up again. Place the blooms in small plastic cups covered with plastic bags to help retain the moisture in the bloom, and store them in a refrigerator. There are more elaborate methods of storing your miniatures. If you have a large plastic container, place a piece of deep Styrofoam in the bottom into which you have cut holes that will hold individual containers. These containers can be small plastic test tubes of the kind used in laboratories or the large plastic tubes used by golfers to hold their clubs, which need to be to about 8 in (20 cm) long.

If you have time, clean up the foliage immediately after cutting. Use a small damp piece of cloth to remove any dirt or insects, and it is a good idea to make sure that you put a name tag on each variety as it is cut. I love the story of the first-time exhibitor who arrived at a show and was not sure of the names of the flowers he had brought along. Three eminent exhibitors looked intently at the roses and agreed on the names. The novice exhibitor hurried away with each flower as the names were written out for him and found later in the day that they had won prizes. He was looking at his winning entries with a worried expression on his face when one of the people who had named the roses asked if there was something wrong. 'Yes,' said the exhibitor, 'these three roses of mine were given different names – but I cut them all from the same bush!'

The main problem for the beginner is knowing just how long it will take some blooms to open, and that is something that comes only with experience. However, if you have some pretty singles that you know will be open and gone before Saturday arrives, cut them while the bud is still tight but showing colour, and put them in the refrigerator. It is best to cut all miniatures as they become available so that you will have lots of blooms to choose from on the morning of the show. Cut the roses early in the morning or late in the evening and drop the stems into a container of tepid water, making sure that you don't get water on the blooms. Florists keep roses soaking in water and refrigerated until they are ready arrange them, and exhibitors can do the same. Remember, too, that varieties will go on growing after they are cut. If blooms are left in rooms that are too warm or in direct sunlight, they will deteriorate far quicker than those stored in cooler temperatures. If, on the night before the show, you find that some varieties you have cut still seem too tight, just take them from the fridge and leave them at normal room temperature overnight.

On the day of the show allow yourself plenty of time at the site. Read the schedule thoroughly – even the most experienced exhibitors make mistakes from over-eagerness – then select the best-looking blooms, clean them and groom them so that they look vibrant and will catch the judging team's eye. The judges are looking for total perfection, and scores are awarded for the following aspects of each rose.

- Bloom form, unless it is stated that the class is for single or open blooms, should be high pointed in a neat circular formation.
- Colour should be true to the variety. Many roses will lose their sparkle after being cut for a day, so the fresher they are the better chance they have of being bright and true.
- Substance is difficult to define, but nobody wants a flabby, lettuce-like bloom.
- Foliage should be clean and free from spray or insect damage. I once had to decide between two roses and finally settled on the one with the better foliage, which upset the other exhibitor who stormed out of the show saying that he thought I was a so-and-so rose judge and not a foliage judge!
- Bloom size should be in relation to the normal growth of the variety; that is, not smaller and not larger than the typical bloom.
- Balance and proportion are best achieved with two or more sets of three- or five-leaflet foliage, but a bloom should not be sacrificed if it has not got these five-leaflet sets. If it is in proportion, it stands as good a chance as the next one.
- When you get a rose with all those points right, then you have the best rose in the show!

If it is a difficult decision for the judges or when it comes to selecting the best bloom or Queen of the Show, it often comes down to what might seem minor points, and this is when the arrangement of the blooms, especially in multi-stem classes, becomes important. Blooms should be evenly matched for both size and form, and colours should be combined so that they do not clash. You do not have to be a qualified flower arranger, but giving an extra thought to the presentation will never be wasted. Presentation should not, however, win over blooms of superior quality.

The following points are likely to diminish your chance of success, especially in classes for individual blooms.

- A bloom that has gone beyond the half-way open stage, except in appropriate classes, that has lost its vibrancy of colour and that has a 'foreign body', which could include a small piece of paper, foam, cotton wool or an aphid, still attached, will be marked down.

- Thick stems with small flowers and spindly stems with large flowers should be avoided. Also try to avoid crooked stems whenever possible; if you have a perfect flower on a slightly crooked stem do not despair, because it could still win although it could be downgraded from the top spot in the show.
- All side buds should be removed in classes for individual blooms, although in classes for sprays, all buds should be left intact.
- Wrong names are likely to lose you points and even disqualify your blooms. Mis-spelling is not now an offence – for instance, you can call a rose 'Kiss and Tell' although the correct name is 'Kiss 'n' Tell'.
- Stem on stem is certain disaster: your main bloom stem should not have part of another stem attached.
- Stems that are too long and that have too much foliage obviously go against the balance and proportion rule. Miniatures on stems that are longer than 6 in (15 cm) are out of proportion, although the arrival of much larger blooms means that this is an area where there will obviously have to be some changes. Even in this case, however, extra long stems and too much foliage would be considered a distraction.

9

THE FUTURE

The future of the miniature rose lies for me in a little part of a garden in mid-California where Ralph Moore plays with pollen in ways that are far in advance of most hybridizers. The man who has been called the father of miniature roses follows his own dictum: 'if you don't dream you will never get anything in roses.'

Moore wants to breed unusual things, and even though he is over 80 years of age, his life and future is filled with the most surprising roses. There are wild roses, old tea roses, the Rugosa and ancient climbers all shuttling for space in the grounds of the nursery that he began in 1937. One of the most important is the Moss rose, which most breeders will not work with because, they say, 'it isn't commercial'. That may be why Ralph Moore works so hard with this rose. The Moss rose, he points out, held a very important place in the old rose world, and there is still a place for it today.

Many of the different roses with which he is hybridizing would surprise most rose breeders. He has produced striped Moss roses and is using the majestic Floribunda/Grandiflora 'Queen Elizabeth' to try to produce a striped, mossed Hybrid Tea. And on the way he is breeding so many lovely mossed varieties that they now have a positive place in the future of the miniature. That future, he hopes, will hold a beautiful crested Moss miniature like *R. centifolia* 'Cristata' (often called 'Chapeau de Napoleon'). He talks about another 10 years to get the fully crested Moss rose among the miniatures.

Whole areas of Moore's nursery are devoted to Rugosa roses, the basic bush with those purple and white large, single flowers that we have all seen in hedgerows throughout the world. Moore has not only miniaturized them, but he has widened the colour range to include reds, pinks, shot silks and even yellow. Not satisfied with that, he has encouraged the rose to produce varieties that will bloom more than once every year, something not thought possible with the original Rugosas. He introduced the first rose from this work, a reblooming yellow Rugosa, in 1987 and called it 'Topaz Jewel'. It was followed a couple of years later by a rounded shrub with miniature foliage that is constantly in flower with pink, white-eyed blooms that are about 2 in (5 cm) across when fully open. This was the first of his new miniature hybrid Rugosas. But now his work with these heavily fragrant old roses has gone far beyond those initial breaks, and the full fruit of his work will not be seen until the mid-1990s. When it is, this group of roses will take on a new significance.

On the benches in his nursery are many, many beautiful roses, some as new as today's sunlight and others from 200 years ago. He breeds with this wide range of roses, all the time looking to their miniature capabilities. Here is 'Old Blush', also called 'Common Monthly', 'Old Pink Daily', 'Old Pink Monthly' and 'Parson's Pink China', that was said to have first been introduced into Sweden in 1752 and into England before 1759. Surely, one would think, in all the years other breeders have tried that same path and brought out everything that 'Old Blush' might have to give. Not as far as Ralph Moore is concerned. He took a direct seedling from this one and found that all the seedlings he got were miniature in size.

However, he also found that sterility was in-built with the miniaturization, but he knows what he wants to get from the rose and believes that the sterility can be overcome.

Every breeder will agree that Ralph Moore introduced the striping back into roses. Before this, the only striping found among roses was in mutation or sports. However, Moore began to use 'Ferdinand Pichard', a rose from 1921, that is of unknown origins but is white splashed with red. From a batch of seedlings he gave the world his little 'Stars 'n' Stripes', the rose that put Sam McGredy on his own path to producing many new striped varieties for the 1990s.

Moore's other great interest is in the introduction of the older Tea roses into the miniature line. When he was a boy his grandfather gave him a plant of a saffron-coloured and fragrant rose called 'Safrano', from 1839. Only now, however, is he bringing it into the breeding line, and almost immediately he has had some success – 'New Adventure' is a direct descendent of 'Safrano'. He gave it that name because he sees it as the start of something totally new and feels that, although it may have been overlooked by other breeders, there are still great possibilities in the rose. He suggests that as it sets seeds other breeders may like to try it for the pollen.

Ruffled blooms in roses are another love, and he is actively breeding for miniatures with totally ruffled petals, another area that few breeders would care to follow. He has also joined the ambitious race to produce a range of roses with a red eye. A red centre to the flower in roses is available only in *R. hulthemosa*, the Persian Rose, and it fascinated the late Scottish breeder, Alec Cocker, who, with Jack Harkness, set about trying to break down its mulish qualities. Jack Harkness succeeded with some early breaks, but the later generations are proving themselves sterile when it comes to breeding. Moore believes that had miniatures been used to cross with *R. hulthemosa* instead of shrubs, more progress would have been made. In the search for something more than the white or yellow eye in the centre of a rose bloom, Moore has taken a totally different approach. Instead of using the Persian Rose he took a small miniature, bred by Sam McGredy, called 'Anytime' and saw that in the centre of its orange blooms there was a distinct purple-like halo. Despite comments from many sources that 'Anytime' never bred anything apart from complete lookalikes, Moore worked and worked, and today he has a range of roses that he calls his halo roses. They are for him only a step away from the full purple or red eye in the rose. And he is already working on a yellow miniature that will have a red or purple eye.

Ask him to generalize about the rose of the future and he will say that there will be a new generation of shrub roses. He believes they will have everything that the average gardener could wish for. They will not be 'exhibition' roses, but will bloom freely, will be easy to grow and care for, be suitable for cutting for low bouquets and other flower arrangements and make good landscape material.

Not only will shrub roses make an impact in miniature roses, so too will a new race of miniature climbing roses. These are not new – again, Ralph Moore was the first to bring in a miniature climber with 'Pink Cameo' – but it is generally agreed that one of the most exciting inputs to the miniatures in recent times has been the arrival of the new climbing miniatures by Chris Warner. They open up all sorts of possibilities and there is no doubt that there will be a commercial opening for these roses and the ones that Warner has lined up to follow them. Breeders will be searching for blooms with the miniature beauty of 'Snow Bride', with a constant repeat of flowers all season long, and on plants that will make rampant climbers.

The question that everyone asks when discussing the future of the rose is: 'What about the blue rose . . . when will it arrive?' In Moore's nursery I recently saw a whole bench devoted to mauve, purple, grey, lavender and lilac roses – but there were no blue ones. There are little roses that are getting closer to that millionaire colour, but the truth is that blue is about the only colour missing from the colour spectrum of the whole rose world, and most hybridizers are pessimistic about the possibility of finding it. For all that, they keep a little corner of their greenhouses free for experiments that might just give us this rose. It does seem more likely that the future of the blue rose lies in the hands of the chemists, who may be able to splice genes to put the missing one into the rose. This is already happening with other flowers, where colours can be modified by gene manipulation. One company has forecast that it can break the blue rose mystery by the mid-1990s, but it would be wonderful if nature itself made the breakthrough, and it would make the first producer a millionaire overnight.

The jet black rose, too, would be something. Already there are some that are so close that it seems that we cannot go any further, but the problem with 'Black Jade' and others like it is that eventually the red that is in them shows through the cloak of black.

There are other colour mixtures hiding out there – chocolate brown, fawn or light brown, and even brown and purple mixed. Texas hybridizer Ernest Williams has a tremendous interest in the brown tones of roses, especially tan-russet shades. In breeding varieties like 'Twilight Trail', 'Smoke Signals', 'Amberglo' and 'Suntan Beauty', he greatly enlarged the availability of these colours, and in producing these roses he has discovered that these colours have brought intense fragrance with them.

Amateur hybridizer Betty Jacobs found much the same when she began to breed through the grey and brown tone roses; her 'Winter Magic' is grey and fragrant. Harmon Saville is also looking at unusual colours with his terracotta shaded 'Teddy Bear' and the lavender with cream reverse, 'Raindrops'.

And what about fragrance? A few years ago one of the aims of the miniature breeders was to put perfume into the miniature, and now not only have Ernest Williams and Betty Jacob achieved this, so too have many other breeders. Now there are several varieties available with every scent you can get from a rose. Everyone loves a truly fragrant rose. The first thing anyone does when you hand them a rose is to smell it, and now the white and mauve miniatures are as generous with their perfumes as the tan, grey and brown varieties. Unfortunately, fragrance is almost as hard to breed into a rose as blue. You can line up four blue-toned roses and finish up with seedlings that are all pink; you can interbreed with four of the most perfumed roses available and not come up with one fragrant seedling. Roses are like that – the hand of man may be the one that spreads the pollen, but it is another that hands out the rewards. The rewards are there – as Ralph Moore has proved – and the future is full of wonderful possibilities still. The dreamers are there to make them all come true, and they will continue to produce wonderful miniature roses, far beyond anything that has yet been accomplished.

IO

RECOMMENDED MINIATURE ROSES

Moss Roses

Where the Moss roses originally came from is another of the mysteries of the rose. What we do know is that the modern Moss miniatures are yet another gift from Ralph Moore. It was just a small part of his research into miniature roses and began with a large rose called 'Golden Moss', which had been bred by Pedro Dot in Spain. From this eventually came the first mossy miniature, the rose red 'Fairy Moss'. Moore's work encouraged other breeders including Jack Christensen and Harmon Saville to produce roses in this style.

There is still a long way to go to achieve the full mossiness that existed in the first roses, the almost bristle-like growth that exuded its own strange fragrance, but Moore believes that breeders 'now have the know-how and the materials . . . all that is needed is the patience and the time to accomplish the goal'. And that goal is for a double, well-formed flower of a good clear colour with well-crested buds on a neat bush.

Among the Moss roses available are: 'Cee Dee Moss' (largish, semi-double, pink flowers); 'Der Carl' (deep pink); 'Dresden Doll' (light pink); 'Elsie Boldick' (medium red); 'Fairy Moss' (medium pink); 'Heidi' (pink); 'Honest Abe' (dark red); 'Honey Moss' (white); 'Jessie Brown' (medium pink); 'Kara' (medium pink); 'Lemon Delight' (medium yellow); 'Mood Music' (striped orange blend); 'Mossy Gem' (medium pink); 'Rose Gilardi' (striped red blend); 'Scarlet Moss' (medium red); 'Single's Better' (medium red); 'Strawberry Swirl' (red blend); 'Toy Balloon' (dark red).

Singles

Single-petalled varieties are not roses with just one petal; they can in fact have 12. In addition, many roses with up to 15 petals – semi-doubles – still look very single, so I have included them here as well so that they are not forgotten. These varieties were overlooked for many years because the public found it difficult to accept something that really looked like a wild rose. There were some large roses – 'Dainty Bess' and 'Altissimo', for example – which, by their very beauty, kept a spot in the world for those with few petals. Now this type of rose is enjoying huge popularity among growers of miniatures, and breeders have produced some lovely varieties.

My own favourite is the yellow 'My Sunshine', for its brightness, the symmetry of its five petals and the glory of its moment of perfection. The trouble with most of these little roses is that their real beauty is fleeting. It was Ralph Moore who began the interest in single-petalled miniatures when he introduced 'Simplex' in 1961; the five petals are white with a golden centre. Later the interest in the type was renewed when Cocker's of Scotland brought in 'Playboy', an orange Floribunda that gathered more fans in the United States than it ever did in Scotland, where it was named 'Cheerio'. British rose breeders have not, in fact, shown a great deal of faith in the single-petalled varieties, but Dickson's of Northern Ireland do have one that will pick up a lot of fans. Called 'Minilights', it is a buttercup yellow and a real eye-catcher.

Most rose shows have a class for the single-petalled miniatures, but they are difficult to show as the main attraction to the judge's eye will be freshness, and this fresh look is hard to maintain. If a room is too hot they can just turn over and disintegrate; if it is too cool they shiver and close up before judging begins. Showing single miniatures is an art in itself. However, their beauty, if fleeting, stays in the memory for a long time. As you may have gathered, I like them, and among my special favourites are: 'Ain't Misbehavin'' (dark red); 'Angel Darling' (mauve); 'Anytime' (orange blend); 'Crazy Dottie' (orange-red blend); 'Cricket' (orange blend); 'Kara' (medium pink); 'Lavender Simplex' (mauve); 'Lavender Star' (lavender-tan); 'Lemon Delight' (medium yellow); 'Little Artist' (red blend); 'Make Believe' (mauve blend); 'Mini-lights' (yellow); 'My Sunshine' (yellow); 'Oriental Simplex' (orange red); 'Peggy T' (medium red); 'Punkin' (orange blend); 'Roller Coaster' (red and white stripes); 'Simplex' (white); 'Single's Better' (medium red); 'Sox' (red blend); 'Stolen Moment' (mauve); 'Wedded Bliss' (medium pink); 'Wee Man' (deep red); 'Why Not' (red blend); 'Zelda Lloyd' (medium pink).

Climbers

Climbing miniatures have not really received the attention of hybridizers until the past few years. It is agreed in many quarters that, if it is only lightly pruned, 'Pompon de Paris' shows all the signs of being a climber, but it is generally kept tightly pruned and so seldom gets the chance to climb. But in 1988 the scene began to change when British hybridizer Chris Warner introduced his climbing miniatures to the rose trade. With one of them, code named Chwizz, now called 'Warm Welcome', he won a Gold Medal, the President's International Trophy and the award for the best rose bred by an amateur all in the Royal National Rose Society's awards in 1988. It was a remarkable achievement, and to prove it was no fluke another of his seedlings was close up in the Certificate of Merit class. Warner's roses flower right through from spring to winter and are very healthy.

In the United States Ralph Moore was also looking at climbers. He introduced a number of new varieties, the most recent being a climbing Moss variety, 'Red Moss Rambler'. A number of other roses have also been introduced as climbers in the United States, but

they are really not more than leggy varieties that seldom reach higher than 4 ft (1.2 m). If a catalogue suggests that you can keep one of these 'climbers' down to ordinary bush size by pruning, ignore the advice and let the rose have its head. The best of the early miniature climbers is certainly the pink 'Jeanne Lajoie'. Others to look out for include: 'Angel Pink' (pink); 'Climbing Orange Sunblaze' (orange); 'Golden Century' (bronze – hard to find); 'Golden Song' (yellow); 'Hi Ho' (deep pink); 'Irish Heart-breaker' (red blend); 'Jazz Time' (deep pink); 'Lavender Mist' (mauve); 'Pink Cameo' (pink); 'Radiant' (orange-red); 'Red Delight)' (red); 'Snowfall' (white); 'Touch o' Midas' (yellow); 'Work of Art' (orange blend).

Micro-miniatures

These are the real tinies of the miniature rose world. 'Si' is still the smallest, but the varieties listed here all produce lovely little flowers and make ideal small rockery plants: 'Baby Betsy McCall' (light pink); 'Bambino' (pink); 'Bit o' Gold' (golden yellow); 'Cinderella' (white); 'Hat Pin' (mauve); 'Little Linda' (yellow); 'Littlest Angel' (yellow); 'Lynn Gold' (yellow); 'Penny Candy' (orange blend); 'Popcorn' (white); 'Red Imp' (medium red); 'Scamp' (velvety red); 'September Days' (deep yellow); 'Si' (light pink); 'Spice Drop' (light pink); 'Stacey Sue' (pink); 'Tiny Flame' (orange red); 'Whiteout' (white); 'Willie Winkie' (light pink).

Hanging Baskets

If you plant a miniature rose in a hanging basket you should choose a rose that trails and has lax growth, although most types of miniature look good in baskets. Whatever variety you select, never let it dry out. The following are among the most suitable varieties: 'Apricot Charm' (apricot); 'Baby Eclipse' (medium yellow); 'Charmglo' (white with pink edge); 'Fresh Pink' (pink); 'Green Ice' (white with greenish tints); 'Jeanne Lajoie' (pink); 'Near You' (light yellow to cream); 'Nozomi' (pearl pink); 'Red Cascade' (dark red); 'Royal Carpet' (bright red); 'Sugar Elf' (pink blend); 'Sweet Chariot' (purple to mauve); 'Swinger' (medium yellow); 'Wedded Bliss' (medium pink).

Cut Flowers

While most miniatures make marvellous bouquets and decorations for the home and will last well in water, not many have become popular with the producers of blooms for the cut-flower market. Many varieties are being tried out, especially those that produce blooms on long enough stems to make good commercial flowers. The list that follows is of varieties capable of giving first-class cut blooms, and it has been produced for me by Ludwig Taschner of South Africa, who is a leading exponent of the value of miniatures as cut flowers: 'Ans' (deep burgundy); 'Astra' (yellow-orange); 'Carmine Button' (carmine pink); 'Coral Button' (coral pink); 'Zwergkönigin' (deep salmon); 'Figurine' (cream); 'Gee Gee' (cream yellow); 'Golden Piccolo' syn. 'Texas' (yellow); 'Imbroglio' (pink and cream); 'Lavender Jade' (lavender); 'Magic Carousel' (white with pink tips); 'Mandola' (medium red); 'Minnie Pearl' (pinkish-cream); 'Old Glory' (orange-red); 'Pacesetter' (white); 'Pirouette' (white-edged carmine-red); 'Party Girl' (apricot); 'Pink Button' (pink); 'Rosaletta' (deep pink veined with silver); 'Salmon Button' (deep salmon); 'Tiny Tot' (light apricot); 'Winsome' (mauve).

Heritage Roses

The return of the old garden varieties has been one of the features of the rose world in recent years. Although these cannot really be described as miniatures, a whole host of the China roses come very close, and they are worth searching out from a grower of old varieties. Many are tender and not suitable for very cold situations, and they love the sun. Here is a short list of the smaller old roses, including the Chinas, that can be used very effectively to back-up your miniature roses, but remember that the blooms are bigger than those on the miniatures.

China Roses

The following are good repeat-flowering varieties in low-growing bushes about 3 ft (0.9 m) high: 'Archduke Charles' (light pink deepening with age); 'Cécile Brunner'(the original Sweetheart Rose, perfect, pale pink buds); 'Comtesse du Cayla' (small, coral to salmon blooms); 'Cramoisi Supérieur' (deep crimson blooms – needs a warm position); 'Colonel Fabvier' (bright crimson with white touches); 'Hermosa' (pink, globular blooms – quite hardy); 'Miss Lowe's Variety' syn. 'Sanguinea' (interesting quilled petals).

Portland Roses

These are generally small, bushy types with neat, full, fragrant flowers, and they are repeat flowering. Consider: 'Arthur de Sansal' (crimson-purple); 'Comte de Chambord' (warm pink, quartered flowers); 'Jacques Cartier' (large flowers on spreading bushes about 3 ft (0.9 m) high); 'Rose de Rescht' (purple-crimson, good repeat-flowering habit); 'The Portland Rose' (light crimson and repeat flowering, grows to about 2 ft (0.6 m).

Bourbon Roses

Hints of the first modern roses can be seen in the Bourbon roses as a result of a great deal of interbreeding between the China, the Portland and other old roses. The flowers are usually heavy and very fragrant. The lowest growing of these is 'Souvenir de la Malmaison', which was named in memory of the great garden lovingly cared for by Empress Josephine. Large flowers, soft pink and fragrant, are borne on a bush that grows to about 3 ft (0.9 m).

Centifolia Roses

These drooping open shrubs could make a good barrier behind a miniature bed if they are sited well back from the modern little roses. The smallest of them is 'De Meaux', which carries miniature-like pink, tightly petalled blooms.

Gallica Roses

Probably the oldest of all garden roses, Gallicas were originally grown by the Greeks and the Romans. There was a great deal of later development and among the lower growing varieties are 'Belle Isis' (flesh pink); 'Cramoisi Picoté' (deep pink pompon); 'Empress Josephine' (large clear pink blooms on a bush that grows about 3 ft (0.9 m) high and wide).

Damask Roses

Damask roses are said to have been brought to Europe from the Middle East by the Crusaders. They make neat bushes, some to only 3 ft (0.9 m) high. Look out for 'Leda' (milky-white), 'Madame Zoetmans' (pale pink) and 'Oeillet Parfait' (warm pink).

Moss Roses

Even though these have been well covered in the modern miniature, some of the originals still make low-growing bushes and might look attractive in a Moss rose garden. Look for 'Alfred de Dalmas' syn. 'Mousseline' (light pink, clusters), 'Japonica' (magenta fading to light lilac-grey), and 'Little Gem' (light crimson and very fragrant blooms, grows to about 2 ft 6 in, 75 cm).

A PERSONAL SELECTION

This is a personal list drawn up over years of growing, judging, breeding miniatures. It includes some of the older varieties that still attract a lot of attention, but there are more of the newer ones for the simple reason that the whole business of growing miniature roses is always reaching towards something new.

I have not attempted to make the constant reference to the size of the blooms, although many of these varieties have been criticized for having blooms that are too big. To many enthusiasts that means a bloom more than $1\frac{1}{2}$ in (4 cm) wide, but there are many beautiful miniatures that should not be passed over because their blooms are a fraction over the accepted size. These larger sized blooms are generally accepted throughout the world in the miniature classification. British growers have established them as Patio roses, and to avoid problems, I have added the Patio roses to my choice as a separate section at the end. I stress that this is for ease of reference and should not be taken as a personal acceptance of the name for the classification, which I consider too limiting.

WHITE TO CREAM

Cinderella   The tiny little flowers on this bushy plant will always excite. 'Cinderella' never knows when to stop blooming, and it is one of the most popular of the early group of roses, having been introduced in 1953 by that Dutch pioneer of miniature roses, Jan de Vink.

Irresistible   Bearing pure white blooms in Hybrid Tea style, 'Irresistible' is being tipped to take over the mantle of top white miniature from 'Snow Bride'. It

is one of the last roses to be hybridized by the talented hands of Dee Bennett.

Popcorn   The one variety that few gardeners would be without, this is a profuse-flowering, short-growing plant. It is unique and looks just like a burst of popcorn. There is a sport available, 'Gourmet Popcorn', which looks very similar but is larger.

Small Virtue   A small rose that is attracting attention for the lovely sprays of white bloom it produces. It loves heat and sunshine.

Snow Bride   This rose from the famous Jolly family of Rosehills Nursery in Maryland is the most beautiful example of purity in a full, perfectly shaped bloom. It constantly wins top awards throughout the world. Blooms can be produced in a large truss or one to a stem, and the centre of each holds a warm touch of cream. It has been justifiably voted number one miniature for a number of years in many parts of the world.

Whiteout   A mass of small, white flowers, touched with pink, are borne in great clusters.

MAUVE–LAVENDER–LILAC

You will not find this colour classification this high in most lists, but I put it here because it is my favourite colour.

Herbie   Rosy-lavender blooms are carried profusely on a loose, sprawling plant, which came from the wonderful hands of the late Dee Bennett. This rose has the class Hybrid Tea shape, and it is winning friends and exhibition prizes just about everywhere. Comparisons should not, I suppose, be made, but 'Herbie' is like a small version of the big rose 'Paradise'.

Lavender Crystal Many roses are said to be 'nearly blue', and here is one that scores in that direction. It is almost a 'might have been' for the most elusive colour of all among roses. The bright yellow stamens catch the eye.

Lavender Jade A rose that carries the high-pointed bloom for which Frank Benerdella's roses are renowned. The reverse of the petals shades from light lavender to white. It produces good flowers that have a delightful fragrance.

Sachet This lively confection of mauve petals with bright yellow stamens opens flat and has a wonderful fragrance.

Smoke Signals Grown by Ernest Williams of Texas, the bush bears smoky-lavender-grey blooms with an intense perfume and exhibition form.

Twilight Trail Another rose from Ernest Williams, this is very unusual in that the colour is registered as a mauve blend – it is actually a mixture of lavender and tan – and it is also fragrant. It received a 'stunning' colour rating.

Winsome Here is the opposite end of the 'mauve colourings' – 'Winsome' is deeper, taking on a lilac-lavender hue. The bloom may be slightly too big for some people, but it is a winner all the way, whether you want it to be admired in your garden or on the show bench.

Winter Magic Another rose with very unusual colouring, 'Winter Magic' is practically grey, with lovely yellow stamens making a fine contrast. It is officially described as light lavender-grey, and it is certainly one on its own. It also has a delightful fragrance.

RED

Acey Duecy This is a rose that is highly regarded everywhere. The medium, bright red blooms have a darker reverse that lifts them to catch the eye. They are carried on a spreading bush.

Beauty Secret One of the early roses from Ralph Moore, 'Beauty Secret' has stayed a favourite since it arrived on the market in 1965. The deep red blooms have good shape and are very attractive.

Black Jade A top 10 rose with a profusion of almost black, perfectly shaped flowers. Alone in its colouring and ability to grow, it went on to win the top award for miniatures in the United States, the Big E for Excellence.

Centerpiece Regarded as one of the better medium reds available, this rose carries well-shaped blooms on a vigorous, compact bush. There are plenty of flowers.

Lady in Red One of my own raising, it carries a lot of exhibition-standard bloom that is red with sometimes a little silvering on the reverse.

Maurine Neuberger An exhibition quality, bright red rose with fully double blooms and a soft fragrance, this variety is going places at a great rate.

Mountie As the name suggests, this is a Canadian rose. It is vigorous but stays well within the size of bloom required by those who want their miniatures within the $1\frac{1}{2}$ in (4 cm) bloom size. The red of the bloom is really bright. 'Mountie' makes a good potted rose.

Nighthawk Red the colour of rubies was how this was described when it won a Big E award in the United States in 1989. The deep red blooms are exhibition form.

Old Glory The medium red petals, with just a touch of yellow at the base, glow. It is another from amateur hybridizer Frank Benerdella, and it also brought him a Big E award.

Red Ace In the United States, the name 'Red Ace' is borne by a currant red rose with good form; the rose grown in Britain under the same name produces magnificent dark crimson, flat-opening blooms. You won't go to a rose show in Britain without seeing it on exhibition there. The British rose was raised by de Ruiter, and it is also known as 'Amruda' and 'Amanda'.

Red Beauty Don't speak a word against this rose to anyone, even if you have found it slightly prone to mildew. Ernest Sheldon, a man who gives away thousands of blooms from his garden of miniatures every year, rates it as everyone's number one, and it is easy to agree with him.

Tara Allison The very bright red, informal blooms make this a constant eye-catcher in the garden. It was named for the daughter of Oregon growers June and Jerry Justice and bred by Sam McGredy.

RED BLENDS

Baby Masquerade   Those who grow and know this great little rose will be surprised to find it here instead of among the yellow blends, but red blend is its official colour classification. I find it far more yellow than red. It is one of the few miniatures introduced by the German hybridizer Tantau. It arrived in 1955 and has been a dazzler ever since.

Debut   A French winner of the top AARS award in 1989, this is a bedding rose *par excellence*. It grows in a mound that seldom gets much higher than 14 in (36 cm). It has great foliage and is a super subject for bedding or for potting. The petals are deep red at the tips, softening to creamy-white at the centre. The flowers are, however, bigger than normal, but for a display rose it will take some beating. It may be available in other countries under another name, so the code name to look for is 'Meibarke'.

Dreamglo   From hybridizer Ernest Williams, this rose has brilliant red and white flowers on a very vigorous, upright bush. It, too, has stood the test of time since its introduction in 1978.

Fancy Pants   Raised by Louisiana hybridizer Gene King, this rose has been highly praised for its colour, profusion of flowers and bloom shape. The bright colour tips the petals with red and then fades through pink to yellow. There is also a spicy fragrance.

Little Artist   A rose from Sam McGredy that is bigger than normal. The informal flowers are borne in profusion and have a lovely fragrance.

Lovers Only   One of my own, the red with a yellow reverse amazed me with its attractiveness when I saw it in full bloom in the Justice nursery in Oregon. A hybridizer really has to wait until he can see his rose grown in numbers to appreciate its qualities. The long-budded blooms are bright and attractive.

Magic Carousel   A rose that cannot be left out of any list, 'Magic Carousel' is a rose that has proved its ability since it was introduced in 1972. It bears a succession of lovely, lace-like blooms in red and white on a bush that can grow tall if left unpruned. But even that is worth trying for the flowers that are produced.

Nickelodeon   If you really want a plant that blooms prolifically with small, white-eyed, red flowers this is for you. Introduced in England in 1989, it really is one to watch.

ORANGE BLEND

Dee Bennett   The flowers are a very pretty apricot and yellow blend, and are borne on a plant that has good shape, substance and an ability to bloom over a long period – which is nothing more than the memory of hybridizer Dee Bennett deserves. It was introduced by a rival breeder, Harmon Saville, in her honour.

Firefly   This vivid bronze-orange rose is from Sam McGredy. It grows strongly and carries lots of small blooms, which makes it an ideal container or garden miniature.

Mary Marshall   Since 1970, this rose, which was named for one of the American Rose Society's most admired rose judges, administrators and growers, has received almost worldwide acclaim. In New Zealand, Australia, India, Canada and the United States it has always been right at the top of the ratings. Unfortunately, when it was brought to Britain it was found to be too prone to mildew for the grower who was offered it. It must have been a mischance because in the years since, this rose has performed well for all those who had early plants of it.

Queen City   Here is one of the most appreciated roses of recent years, being rated number two in the 1988 American Rose Society survey, one year after it was introduced by Suzy and Dennis Bridges. It is orange with a yellow base and fades to a lighter colour. The flowers are usually carried one to a stem. Its immediate future seems assured.

Sunny Sunblaze   This is a difficult rose to place as its blooms vary from a mixture of light cream and orange to white; its official description, however, is orange blend. It is one of the great range of roses sold in Europe by the Meilland firm. All bear the names 'Sunblaze' or 'Meillandina', the two group names selected for the sale of the Patio and miniature roses, and they are generally sold under their colour designation, such as orange, apricot, red and apricot. Although they are mostly bred by the Meilland family, the company does select other growers' roses with the result that 'Golden Sunblaze' is also 'Rise 'n' Shine' and 'Apricot Sunblaze' is 'Mark One'.

ORANGE-RED

Chattem Centennial   The brightest of all the orange-red plants that I have seen, 'Chattem Centennial' is a constant bloomer. The flowers are flattish, and this rose deserves a place where a bright, vigorous but true miniature is needed. It was one of the first of many successful roses introduced by Nelson Jolly.

Chris Jolly   Here is a really lovely rose that is truly on the borderline between miniature (large) and Floribunda. A superbly coloured rose, it deserves a place where a taller growing plant with a large flower would be useful.

Darling Flame   One of Europe's most successful miniatures since its introduction in 1971, it is a plant that blooms well and heavily, with a pretty but informal flower. It comes from Meilland in France, the producers of that other top miniature 'Starina'. This is also known as 'Minuetto'.

Pucker Up   Although it is variable in colour, from orange-red to deep red, it is a real winner. The plant can become rather lanky, but it has good disease resistance.

Razzmatazz   If you want a rose that flowers and flowers and flowers, this is for you. The blooms may not have much shape, but they are always there!

Starina   Little can be said to add to the worldwide praise for this French-bred rose, which has stood its ground against all opposition since 1965. The luminous orange-red blooms have a hint of yellow at the base.

PINK

Angela Rippon   You may see this rose as 'Ocarina' or 'Ocaru', but it seems to be well-known throughout the world carrying the name of the TV personality. It is very hard to find in the United States or Canada, where only one nursery to my knowledge carries it – Heirloom Roses of St Pauls, Oregon. It came into Britain through Fryers of Knutsford in 1979, and it has continued to be a big seller, rating number one spot in the annual analysis of the Royal National Rose Society. Ludwig Taschner says that 'it may be considered the best miniature to date'. I would recommend it anywhere as a fine garden plant.

Cupcake   The colour was called pink frosting, and that is what it is – a soft, pink, long-lasting bloom on a vigorous bush.

Funny Girl   This rose has been praised to the skies for its ability to grow in the garden where the informal and loose blooms can be fully appreciated.

Kinggig   This good-looking rose bears flowers that are a mixture of pinks. Its tradename is 'Giggles', which is a far better name of course, but it is officially registered as 'Kinggig', from the hybridizer Gene King of Louisiana. The high-centred bloom is ideal for exhibition although some will say that it comes a little too large. That should not prevent it from having a lot of fans for its disease resistance, reliability in blooming and vigour.

Madelaine Spezzano   'Too big', was the cry when Dee Bennett introduced this lovely variety in 1985. But despite the cries, it still managed, with its colour, form and substance, to make the 1988 top 10 list.

Marty's Triumph   This light pink rose has slowly worked its way to the top since its introduction by the Bischoffs in 1984. Its exhibition potential is highly regarded.

Peggy Jane   There has to come a time in your life when you step out of line with general opinion, and that has to be my stance here. I have watched this little rose for a few years, and it produces masses of lovely pink blooms, but it seems that few people like a plant that hugs the ground like this one and that does not have stems long enough for cutting. Put it in a tub and see the sight it makes.

Pierrine   The medium pink blooms are full, high centred and carried one to a stem. Although it was introduced only in 1988, it has made considerable progress to the top of the list of roses for showing. A recommendation from the American Rose Society's Roses in Review 1990 by Fred Wenzel says that 'even if you don't grow minis you should have this beauty'. There can't be a much higher recommendation than that.

Tipper   A 1989 winner of the Big E award, this is a medium-to-large miniature from Jollys of Rosehill Farm. The long-lasting flowers are in soft shades of pink.

PINK BLEND

Jennifer Although 'Jennifer' is registered as pink, there is such delicacy about the colour that it looks more like a very soft mauve with a lighter reverse. I saw it when it was just a seedling in Frank Benerdella's New Jersey garden, and it seemed mauvish with a lighter reverse then – and it still does. It is perfect in bud and at all stages of bloom.

Kitty Hawk Although this rose is often described as too big, it is becoming widely accepted, and it may be that all the larger miniatures will get their just place eventually. Certainly this ones deserves it, if only for the perfection of the blooms, which are borne singly. It is almost full pink, but there is a slightly lighter pink on the reverse of the petals. It might need extra attention if blackspot is around.

Minnie Pearl This is a lovely flower if only it would hold its light pink colouring. In many places, unfortunately, it tends to be almost white with pink tipping on the edges. It is a top exhibition rose, which is only right as it is named for a top entertainer on the Grand Ole Opry show from Nashville, Tennessee.

Peaches 'n' Cream Pink blend is the official colouring of this first-class miniature but in many areas it comes out almost white. The breeder, Ernest Woolcock, gave me the opportunity of propagating it and giving plants to many growers in Britain, with the result that it is now on many growers' lists and is consistently named as a very good show rose.

Tiffany Lynn Another of the in-between varieties, 'Tiffany Lynn' is still beautiful enough to win over anyone. It has lovely flower form, and the blooms are medium to deep pink with a whitish reverse.

YELLOW

Center Gold Another biggest bloom but one that is always an eye-catcher, even when it happens to throw a pure white flower on the same bush. A really lovely cut flower, 'Center Gold' wins many prizes on the show bench.

Freegold One of the miniatures to come from New Zealand's Sam McGredy, who is better known for his brilliance at producing big roses, this is a deep yellow with fine substance in the petals. It is sold in Britain as 'Penelope Keith'.

June Laver If ever I was stunned by the beauty of one bloom on a rose this was the one that did it. Hybridized by the Laver family in Canada, it is destined for a top place on the show bench, even though the stems underneath the medium-to-large flowers are quite short. It is a deep yellow that ages to a pretty cream.

Lemon Twist From the lady who gave us 'Winter Magic', Betty Jacobs, this deep yellow, 25-petalled bloom has a high-centred, exhibition-style flower on a bushy plant.

Luis Desamero This rose is named for one of California's top exhibitors, and indeed, it has all that a show rose should have – shape, vigorous growth and plenty of exhibition, high-pointed blooms. I had included it in the white section of this listing when I discovered that it is really registered as a medium yellow. Yet in my garden it is almost white with just a light touch of yellow near the centre. Whatever the shade, it is a fine rose.

Olympic Gold Here is the perfect answer to those who say they don't like large miniatures. This one can grow large, but the flowers and foliage stay fully in proportion.

Rise 'n' Shine There is still no challenger, in my opinion, for this great growing, bright yellow, disease-free (well, as disease-free as you can get) variety. Introduced in 1977, it was good enough in the 1980s to be re-named 'Golden Sunblaze' in Europe. It is possible to see the two roses sold side by side as different varieties!

Sequoia Gold This may be the rose that will take over from 'Rise 'n' Shine'. It is produced by the same breeder, Ralph Moore, and won an Award of Excellence in 1987. It holds its colour better than most yellows and is produced in clusters, occasionally with one to a stem, that often has a high-pointed, exhibition-style centre.

Sunshine Girl This rose produces a bigger bloom than the other yellows mentioned here, but that should not be held against it. It comes from the hybridizing of Ernest Woolcock, who gave the world the lovely 'Peaches 'n' Cream'.

Texas Flowers are a strong unfading yellow on this rose from Poulsen's of Denmark. It is also known as 'Golden Piccolo', and it is an upright grower with long, pointed buds and semi-double blooms. The vigorous bush grows to about knee-height, which probably takes it into the larger-than-miniature category.

YELLOW BLEND

Party Girl The colour varies quite a bit, from yellow to apricot, but that should not bother those who love a well-shaped bloom with lots of substance.
Rainbow's End This rose is a great all-rounder. In the sun, the blooms are edged with a carmine-red but if grown in a shady spot they can often come up pure yellow.
Tracey Wickham Probably the only Australian miniature rose to make any impression in the class, 'Tracey Wickham' comes from New South Wales, where Eric Welsh has been breeding roses for some years. Its red and yellow blooms have made a great impression in the United States as well as in Australia.

APRICOT BLEND

Free Spirit Here is a rose that lives up to its name. It is really free with its flowering, it is a vigorous grower, and the flowers are of exhibition quality. The American Rose Society's annual analysis described it as 'easy to grow'.
Holy Toledo A long-time favourite of mine, this rose bears well-shaped blooms on a leggy plant, but the flowers more than make up for the ungainly growth. It is also a wonderful rose to give as a gift to a friend as every cutting takes without the slightest problem.
Jean Kenneally What can anyone say about one of the most popular roses for years in the United States? The blooms are perfection – the perfect size and the perfect shape on an upright bush. The colour may fade, and in some places it will need just a little extra care if mildew arrives, but even this will not detract from a lovely rose, which is named for a top Californian rose judge.
Loving Touch If the term Macro-miniature is ever introduced, this is one rose that can be so described. It carries a wonderfully shaped flower that sometimes, unfortunately, fades and dips in the centre, but there are lots of blooms. The plant grows tall and has an occasional disease problem – but even these failings

cannot really take away from what is a superb rose.
Sara Robinson True apricot, fragrant flowers are borne on a well-proportioned plant. This is one of a number of recent roses to come from Guernsey grower, Thomas Robinson, a descendent of the man who introduced the de Vink roses to Britain. Among his other excellent roses are 'Dollie B', 'Ginny-Lou' and 'Woodlands Lady'.
Susan Noel The very full bloom – of 80 petals – is a light apricot, almost a pastel shade. The blooms are well shaped, and the plant grows well.

STRIPED VARIETIES

I feel that these roses should be listed separately. If they appear under other headings, such as the blends, those who like some variety in their gardens might miss them altogether. You could call them novelties, but they certainly will give a lift to your beds or, when grown in pots, to the patio.
Earthquake This bears masses of full flowers in red, orange and yellow stripes. No two blooms will ever be alike.
Pandemonium A well-named rose for it bears a riot of red, orange and yellow-striped flowers that make a devastating impression. If you want something to catch people's attention, this rose is for you. It is called 'Claire Rayner' in Britain.
Pinstripe This has been called the best of the striped roses, but that is obviously a personal judgement. The small blooms are red with white stripes, but you seldom find two blooms alike. The plant has a low, mounded habit.
Roller Coaster A rose that almost fits in with the singles, for the blooms sometimes have only six petals, although some have up to 14. The flowers are a blend of red and white stripes and have a slight fragrance.
Rose Gilardi Lovely, slightly mossed buds open out to pretty flowers in red, pink and white stripes. If it is grown out of the sun, it can have the added novelty of many broader white stripes.
Stars 'n' Stripes This is the variety that really began striping in roses. The initiator was Ralph Moore, but since its introduction in 1975 this red and white rose has been used by other breeders, who willingly acknowledge the influence of this variety,

which has a good repeat-flowering habit as well as a soft fragrance.

Whistle Stop This vigorous plant carries blooms of magenta and white as well as a spicy fragrance.

PATIO ROSES

In this section I have selected only the roses that have been given this classification in Britain. In the United States, Canada and several other important rose growing areas, these roses are still regarded as miniatures simply because there is no official classification of Patio. In the United States an effort was made to call them Sweetheart roses, but the name never really caught on. Whatever they are called, they deserve a more positive place in the world of the rose, but before you plant one, do try to find out what its ultimate height will be.

Anna Ford Orange-red blooms with bright yellow centres are borne on short, spreading growth. It is now being used extensively for breeding.

Buttons This rose is one of many that you will find in this list from Pat Dickson of Northern Ireland, who has practically made the Patio list his own. The well-shaped blooms are a light salmon-red.

Cider Cup I find this one of the most attractive of the Dickson roses. The deep apricot blooms are a wonderful shape, and the plant never stops flowering.

Clarissa Trusses of lovely apricot blooms are borne on a tallish, upright bush that was bred by Jack Harkness, who has been responsible for a batch of new miniatures recently.

Conservation This rose from Cockers of Scotland carries pretty salmon-red, almost orange blooms and has a good growing habit.

Gentle Touch The buds have a lovely miniature shape, but the fully open, pale pink blooms are large.

Ginger Nut The bronze-orange petals have a deeper reverse, and the informal, double blooms are borne on a compact bush.

Little Woman Salmon to rose-pink, well-shaped blooms are carried on this rose from South Africa, which is said to grow 'like a miniature climber'.

Minilights The single flowers are yellow, and the foliage is bright. It makes a spreading plant.

Peek-a-boo Known as 'Brass Ring' in catalogues in the United States, this has apricot flowers. It is low spreading and makes a lovely tree or half-standard subject.

Ray of Sunshine Semi-double, bright yellow blooms are carried in clusters of five to seven flowers.

Scottish Special Soft pinky-peach flowers with bright yellow stamens are borne over a long period.

Save the Children A compact and bushy plant with deep scarlet flowers that have a touch of gold at the base of the petals.

Sweet Magic The orange and golden blooms are small and well formed but, like so many in this class, the final flower opens wide.

Tear Drop The white flowers have a yellow eye and are carried in clusters, which although they vanish quickly, do have a good repeat.

TOP RATED

The following are the top-rated miniature roses by the American Rose Society as published in their 1991 Handbook for Selecting Roses. This means that the roses all scored 8.0 or higher from a top mark of 10.

Colour Blends
'Baby Darling', 'Dreamglo', 'Holy Toledo', 'Jean Kenneally', 'Kathy Robinson', 'Little Artist', 'Little Jackie', 'Magic Carousel', 'Mary Marshall', 'Minnie Pearl', 'Over the Rainbow', 'Party Girl', 'Peaches 'n' Cream', 'Puppy Love', 'Rainbow's End', 'Rosmarin', 'Toy Clown', 'Winsome'.

Pink
'Baby Betsy McCall', 'Cuddles', 'Cupcake', 'Fresh Pink', 'Judy Fischer', 'Kinggig', 'Swedish Doll', 'Willie Winkie'.

Red
'Beauty Secret', 'Kathy', 'Rose Hills Red', 'Sheri Anne', 'Starina', 'Top Secret'.

White
'Cinderella', 'Little Eskimo', 'Popcorn', 'Simplex', 'Snow Bride', 'Starglo'.

Yellow
'Rise 'n' Shine', 'Yellow Doll'.

BIBLIOGRAPHY

My interest in miniature roses, which began many years ago, has brought me into contact with a great deal of material written over the past 150 years. I have consulted a wide range of publications, initially from mere interest but later to verify information for this book. Surprisingly, miniature roses have not had anything like the exposure given to other areas of rose growing, and there are few books available dealing specifically with them. Those that have come my way are *Miniature Roses*, which was published in New Zealand by Dawn and Barry Eagle; *A New Zealand Guide to Miniature Roses* by Margaret Hayward; *The Complete Book of Miniature Roses* by Charles Marden Fitch; and, the first of them all, *Miniature Roses* by Roy Genders, which was published in 1960. Ralph Moore has produced some small books, but his real story has still to be told. There was also my previous book on the subject *Miniature Roses for Homes and Garden* (David & Charles, 1985). Since all these books were published, the rise of the miniature rose has continued at a great pace, and descriptions of the methods of working with them, as well as the endless stream of new varieties, need updating.

For anyone who wishes to research the story of the miniature I would suggest the following areas: rose annuals and other publications from the Royal National Rose Society, the American Rose Society, the New Zealand Rose Society, the Australian Rose Society and the Canadian Rose Society. The quarterly journal *Florettes* (previously entitled *The Miniature Rose Growers Bulletin*), which is edited by Luis T. Desamero for the American Rose Society (PO Box 30,000, Shreveport, Louisiana 71130). This is an invaluable publication that contains up-to-date information on every aspect of miniature rose growing.

The sections devoted to miniatures in most modern rose books, especially *Roses* by Jack Harkness; *Rose Growing Complete* by E. B. Le Grice; *Modern Roses* by Peter Harkness; *Look to the Rose* by Sam McGredy; *The Book of the Rose* by Michael Gibson; and, for identification purposes, *Roses* by Roger Phillips and Martyn Rix.

The Combined Rose List, an annual publication from Beverly R. Dobson, 215 Harriman Road, Irvington, New York 10533, is considered the international 'bible' of rose growers and covers the world-wide availability of roses. For British growers, the annual publication *Find that Rose* (published by the Rose Growers Association) increases in its scope and presentation every year and is available from the Editor, Angela Pawsey, 303 Mile End Road, Colchester, Essex CO4 5EA, England.

INDEX